BIBLICAL

MARRIAGE

Dave Earley

Dave Earley Ministries
1972 Tournament Way
Grove City, OH 43123
702-540-0334

Printed in the United States of America.
For Worthwhile Books Publications
Columbus, Ohio

Contents

Dedication

To Cathy,
I fell in love with you the first time I saw you
and have been in love with you ever since.
Loving you just keeps getting better and better. Thanks for being my
corresponding compliment, parenting partner, ministry colleague, soul
mate, girlfriend, lover, and very best friend.

Introduction:
Consult the Marriage Expert

You want to be happily married.

You want to have the type of marriage that God will gladly bless.

You hope to love and be loved in a strong covenant that holds through tough times.

Of course you do. We all do.

And you can. But you need to go at it God's way.

Let me make a couple of things clear right from the start.

First, even though I've been fortunate enough to be married for thirty years and have read plenty of excellent books and articles on marriage, and even though I have a degree in counseling and have done my share of marriage counseling, I do not consider myself an expert on marriage. There is only one true expert, and that's God.

God designed marriage. And He created men and women. As the only eternal and everywhere-present (omnipresent) being, He has seen every marriage in history. And He alone fully understands marriage. With such an expert available, why search elsewhere?

Second, God has not kept His expertise to Himself. He has generously shared His knowledge with us in the Bible. This amazing book speaks with astounding clarity and incredible accuracy on dozens of subjects, including marriage.

Woven through the life lessons that grace the pages of the Bible are timeless, fundamental, proven principles that have served as the building blocks of successful marriages for thousands of years. I call them "secrets" because, in today's world, these principles are tragically overlooked and under-applied.

There are many fine books that emphasize one or two of these secrets and help us wisely apply them, but the secrets alone will not be as effective unless we start by understanding the underlying biblical principles.

This book distills what the Bible says about marriage into fourteen practical principles that are guaranteed to improve your marriage. Whether you are just starting out, are going through a rough patch in the middle, or are looking to finish strong, these fourteen secrets, *if properly applied*, will help you become a better marriage partner.

Suggestions for a More Effective Marriage

No matter where your marriage stands, from very good to awful, it *can* be improved. I suggest the following approach to make sure your marriage moves forward:

1. Read this book by yourself and prayerfully ask God to work these fourteen secrets into your life.

I suggest that you read it slowly, with a pen in hand, marking key ideas and making notes in the margins. Try to put into practice what you are learning. Ask God to help you apply what you've read.

2. Read this book with your mate or mate-to-be.

Read one chapter at a time, at most. Take turns reading it aloud. Stop after each section and discuss what you *think*, what you *feel*, and how you can *apply* what you've read.

3. Read this book as part of a small group.

Get with a group of other couples. Study one chapter at a time. Discuss how you are striving to live out these truths in real life. Pray for one another.

4. Reread this book annually, by yourself and with your mate.

Chapter 1

Build on a Solid Foundation

It was the middle of May, the sky was a brilliant blue, the sun was in full array, the birds were happily singing, and the hills were lush and green. I was standing in the sanctuary of a little red brick church at a wide place in the road charmingly named Sweet Valley, Pennsylvania. The room was filled with flowers, smiling faces, and beautiful music. My best friends were standing nervously on my left in black tuxedos; two smiling pastors flanked me on my right as my mom and dad sat in the front pew grinning up at me. All was good—but it quickly got much better.

The organ burst forth in Wagner's "Bridal Chorus." Everyone rose to their feet and all eyes turned to the back of the church, where a distinguished, but anxious, man in a blue suit stood with a young lady in a white dress clinging eagerly to his arm. Wow! She was gorgeous. Her smile illuminated the room. Best of all, her eyes locked with mine and her smile got even bigger.

Yes! I thought. *She's going to be mine.*

But when Cathy and her father were about halfway down the aisle, another thought hit me: *Whoa, this is a really big deal. She's counting on me to take care of her.* I gulped. *This is a big responsibility. I better not mess this up.*

That was nearly thirty years ago. I'm happy to say that God has blessed us and we have made our marriage work. But, sadly, for half the couples who get married in the United States each year, their marriages won't work out.

What Happened?

If we look at the history of marriage in the United Sates, we see a troubling picture. Divorce used to be the exception, but this is no longer the case. As recently as 1920, only one out of seven marriages ended in divorce. That means 86 percent of the marriages lasted. By 1940, the number of divorces had jumped to one out of six, meaning that 83 percent now went the distance. The divorce rate rose to one out of four marriages by 1960, and escalated to one out of three by 1972. Since 1985, one out of two marriages has ended in divorce; in other words, only 50 percent of the people who get married stay married.

What happened?

Though several factors have contributed to the rise in the divorce rate, the most obvious is that America has become increasingly secular. More and more people approach marriage without a biblical view of what God intended marriage to be. By failing to build on a biblical foundation for marital fulfillment, they set themselves up for disillusionment, heartache, and defeat.

The Foundation

I never valued the importance of a strong foundation until we built our first church auditorium. I was shocked when the bids came in. Hundreds of thousands of dollars would go into work that no one would ever see. Aside from the obvious concrete, huge pipes, long cables, and deep footers had to go in underground before we could even begin to build what everyone would see. When I was tempted to fudge a bit on the foundation, a wise architect cautioned me: "Nothing is more important than the foundation."

Through the process of building that worship center and a few other buildings, I learned the immense value of a good foundation.

1. *A good foundation is essential for the health and well-being of a building.* It is also essential for the health and well-being of a marriage.

2. *A building cannot withstand much stress or pressure without a solid foundation.* Likewise, a marriage cannot withstand the storms of life without a solid foundation.

3. *A building's strength depends proportionally on the strength of its foundation.* The strength of a marriage depends on the quality of its foundation.

4. *The greater a building's height, the greater the importance of its foundation.* The higher you want your marriage to go, the greater the importance of the foundation.

5. *The foundation of a great building is not readily visible, yet it is essential.* The foundation of your marriage will not be immediately noticeable, yet it is essential for the strength, growth, and quality of your marriage.

Secret #1
Build on a solid foundation.

In Hebrew, the word *genesis* means "beginning." Everything about creation and life begins in the book of Genesis—including plants, animals, humanity, sin, redemption, government, and marriage. In fact, as early as the second chapter of Genesis, the story of marriage begins to unfold. Read this well-known story slowly:

> Then the LORD God said, "It is not good for the man to be alone;
> I will make him a helper suitable for him." Out of the ground the LORD
> God formed every beast of the field and every bird of the sky, and brought
> them to the man to see what he would call them; and whatever the man
> called a living creature, that was its name. The man gave names to all
> the cattle, and to the birds of the sky, and to every beast of the field,
> but for Adam there was not found a helper suitable for him.
> So the LORD God caused a deep sleep to fall upon the man, and he slept;
> then He took one of his ribs and closed up the flesh at that place.
> The LORD God fashioned into a woman the rib which He had taken
> from the man, and brought her to the man. The man said,
> "This is now bone of my bones, and flesh of my flesh;
> she shall be called Woman, because she was taken out of Man."
> For this reason a man shall leave his father and his mother, and be joined
> to his wife; and they shall become one flesh. And the man
> and his wife were both naked and were not ashamed.
>
> GENESIS 2:18–25 NASB

The last two sentences are quoted elsewhere in the Bible—by Jesus in Matthew 19:5–6 and Mark 10:7–9; and by Paul in 1 Corinthians 6:16–17 and Ephesians 5:31. Jesus added these very important words: "So they are no longer two, but one flesh. What therefore God has joined together let no man separate" (Matthew 19:6; Mark 10:8–9 NASB).

From these familiar words, we can discern the foundational stones of a strong marriage. Throughout the rest of this book, we will see how the Bible builds on the foundation laid down succinctly in the opening chapters of Genesis.

1. Recognize God as the expert.

"It is not good for the man to be alone" (Genesis 2:18 NASB). As you may recall, at the close of the sixth day of Creation, God surveyed everything He had made and pronounced it "very good" (Genesis 1:31). But then God said that something in His beautiful world was *not* good— the man was alone.

So God resolved to act. He said, "I will make him a helper suitable for him" (Genesis 2:18 NASB). Here we see that marriage was God's idea. God had previously created the first man. Now He created the first woman. From the man's side, God crafted a woman. Then, like a proud father on his daughter's wedding day, God brought the woman to Adam and gave her to him. In other words, God created the first marriage— which makes Him the expert. His Word now serves as our foundation for understanding marriage.

2. Focus on companionship.

Unlike the pairs of animals he named, Adam was alone. There was no corresponding complement for him. God declared that the situation was not good. Adam needed a companion.

Marriage was not created merely so the human race would reproduce offspring. It was founded by God to meet the human need for companionship.

People who enjoy strong marriages focus on companionship. Healthy marriage is built on more than physical attraction, romance, and sex. Long marriages result as couples learn to develop a deep friendship with one another.

3. Complement each other.

"I will make him a helper suitable for him." The phrase "helper suitable for him" literally means "a help opposite him" or "corresponding to him." The idea is a helping counterpart; a corresponding complement; connecting pieces that fit together. God created husbands and wives to be positive counterparts.

"The LORD God fashioned into a woman the rib which He had taken from the man" (Genesis 2:22 NASB). Woman came from man's side. As Matthew Henry observes, she was "not made out of his head to rule over him, nor out of his feet to be trampled upon by him, but out of his side to be equal with him, under his arm to be protected, and near his heart to be beloved."[1]

"'This is now bone of my bones, and flesh of my flesh; she shall be called Woman' " (Genesis 2:23 NASB). In the original language, Adam's words are a joyous declaration. While he obviously enjoyed the other animals, he was thrilled when he saw Eve. He recognized that she was like him. Though uniquely female, she looked like him, talked like him, walked like him, and smiled like him. She was his complement. He could relate to her as to no other living creature. She was another human being. God designed husbands and wives to be close friends and to positively complement one another as they work together side by side as equal partners and close companions.

4. Prioritize the relationship.

Note that God created marriage to be a union between a man and a woman—not a man and another man or a woman and another woman. Note also that God designed marriage to be a union between one man and one woman—not one man and several women, or one woman and several men.

Adam and Eve had a sole focus—each other. Eve was the only woman in Adam's life, and he was the only man in hers. This is instructive for us. Couples with strong marriages place their marriage relationship above all other human relationships. Second only to their relationship with God, their mate is the most important thing in their lives.

5. Husbands need to step up and lead.

Of the two, men and women, the man was created first. The woman was made from the man. The woman was brought to the man. Then the man was given the authority to name the woman. Also, it was the man who was commanded to leave his father and his mother and be joined to his wife. What does all that add up to? It shows that it was God's intent for the husband to give leadership to the marriage and the family.

This has nothing to do with men and women having different worth. It has everything to do with husbands and wives having different roles. As we shall see, the Bible makes it clear that God expects husbands to step up and selflessly give leadership to their homes.

6. Form an independent union.

"For this reason a man shall leave his father and his mother" (Genesis 2:24 NASB). The idea of "leaving" father and mother is not that of utterly forsaking them. Rather, it is the notion of establishing a new adult relationship, a new family unit that has its own physical, financial, and emotional independence.

No one is ready to get married until he or she is able to live emotionally, financially, and physically independent of his or her parents. A marriage becomes stronger as a couple learns to make it on their own, without Mom and Dad.

7. Bond to each other.

The man was not only told to leave his father and mother, but also to "be joined to his wife." The point of separating from his parents was to unite with his wife. *Joined* carries the idea of being "glued to" or "cemented together." In fact, the same word in Hebrew is used to describe how leprosy would *cling to* the skin of the wicked servant Gehazi (2 Kings 5:27); that is, to become part and parcel with his being. Obviously, marriage is not a disease, like leprosy. But the idea is that marriage partners must bond to each other as tightly as leprosy clings to the skin of the one it infects. Unfortunate comparison, but you get the picture.

I've heard that if you glue together two pieces of plywood, they become five times stronger than each piece would be on its own. (That's a better analogy!) Good marriages are the result of two independent adults clinging tightly to each other. Both are strengthened individually as they bond their lives together.

8. Develop deep intimacy.

The goal of marriage is that husbands and wives would "become one flesh." Obviously, this speaks of the deep physical oneness that comes when joining in sexual intercourse. The Apostle Paul's description of this oneness in 1 Corinthians 6:15–16 refers to sexual union. It is possible to create a degree of oneness with someone other than your mate through the act of sexual intercourse—which is one reason the Bible clearly forbids engaging in fornication and adultery.

In God's eyes, the act of intercourse makes a man and a woman "one flesh." It creates a powerful bond. But truly becoming "one flesh" in marriage involves much more than physical intimacy. Sexual intercourse is designed to be *only a beginning* point in the great adventure of getting to know each other. True unity and oneness are yet in the future for a newly married couple. The unveiling and joining together of our bodies is symbolic of the emotional and spiritual openness and interconnection that God designed for couples to enjoy in marriage. As a couple develops emotional and spiritual oneness, their physical intimacy will be enhanced and deepened. Good sex without a good relationship will not enhance marital unity; but a good relationship will enhance sex and build marital unity. Deep intimacy is achieved as a couple grows together physically, emotionally, and spiritually. It involves a process that takes time, insight, sensitivity, and effort.

9. Be vulnerable and accepting.

"And the man and his wife were both naked and were not ashamed" (Genesis 2:25 NASB). What a beautiful picture of openness, vulnerability, and innocence! The lack of shame reflects the truth that the only place for sexual activity is within the bounds of marriage. The author of Hebrews reminds us that "marriage is honorable among all, and the bed undefiled; but fornicators and adulterers God will judge"

(Hebrews 13:4 NKJV). Within the covenant of marriage, sexual activity is pure, beautiful, and honorable. Outside of marriage, sexual activity is corrupted, dirty, and shameful.

The notion of being "naked and not ashamed" also speaks to a deeper issue of vulnerability and acceptance. True intimacy is achieved when a husband and wife feel the freedom to be completely honest, open, genuine, and authentic with each other. It occurs as they share their deepest hopes, dreams, fears, and secrets without fear of rejection.

10. Tear down relational walls.

In Genesis 2, the paradise of innocence is created. In Genesis 3, it is lost.

> *They heard the sound of the* LORD *God walking in the garden in the cool of the day, and Adam and his wife hid themselves from the presence of the* LORD *God among the trees of the garden. Then the* LORD *God called to Adam and said to him, "Where are you?" So he said, "I heard Your voice in the garden, and I was afraid because I was naked; and I hid myself."*
>
> GENESIS 3:8–10 NKJV

After sin entered the picture, Adam and Eve were no longer innocently "naked and unashamed." They were guilty and guarded. The greatest barrier to deep relational unity is unresolved relational sin, such as harshness, neglect, dishonesty, criticism, failure to communicate, and unfair fighting. The only way to break down the barriers created through such sins is humble, honest, sincere confession and forgiveness.

11. Rely on the third party.

Marriage is much more than a legal contract between two people. When Jesus said, "What therefore *God* has joined together, let not man separate" (Matthew 19:6 ESV, emphasis added), He established that marriage is a covenantal work of God, whereby He Himself enters into the union and pledges His help and support. What a marvelous encouragement! No couple has to go it alone. God Himself is ready, willing, and able to lend His wisdom, guidance, and strength.

12. Determine to make it permanent.

Note that Jesus' statement also comes with a stern warning: "let no man separate." Marriage was intended to be a permanent union. Successful marriages begin when both the husband and wife enter into the covenant with the understanding that divorce is not an option.

Notes

1. Matthew Henry, *Commentary on the Whole Bible,* vol. 1 (Grand Rapids, MI: Christian Classics Ethereal Library, 2000), 41.

Chapter 2

Fulfill Your Vows

On that beautiful spring day when Cathy wore the long white dress and the big smile and we stood before a church full of people, we said some sacred words. We held hands, looked into each other's eyes, and promised

> *To have and to hold,*
> *From this day forward,*
> *For better, for worse,*
> *For richer, for poorer,*
> *In sickness and in health,*
> *To love and to cherish,*
> *Till death do us part.*

Then we exchanged rings and vowed, "With this ring I thee wed, and with all my worldly goods I thee endow." Of course, all the "worldly goods" we had were a couple of boxes of books, some very inexpensive clothes, a 1979 white Ford Pinto hatchback with a red racing stripe, and nine hundred dollars in cash we received as wedding gifts. That was it, but we gladly pledged it to each other.

As I write this, I find it hard to believe that Cathy and I were married thirty years ago. Time flies. I remember as if it were yesterday watching her walk down the aisle. So much has happened in the last thirty years. Much has been "better," a few things "worse." For the longest time, we were "poorer," but lately we have become "richer"—though we have always been "richer" in the things that matter most. We have endured some very serious "sickness," and some blessed "health." Through it all, we have "loved and cherished" each other. . .most of the time.

We quickly discovered that we didn't know the other as well as we thought. In all honesty, marriage was much harder than either of us expected. After launching a new church and fathering three children in four years, I got extremely sick with a life-dominating chronic illness. That made the normal stresses of marriage, ministry, and three little children that much more difficult. Not to mention the constraints of a very tight income. Cathy and I could each tell you of times when it felt as if just calling it quits and walking away would have been so much easier than persevering.

But we had made those vows. We had promised "until death do us part." So we hung in there—and we've always been glad we did.

Biblical marriage is a sacred covenant between three people: a man, a woman, and God. It is a very serious commitment. Families, societies, and nations are built on it. A strong marriage is the result of a husband and a wife dedicating themselves to fulfill their vows.

Secret #2
Fulfill your vows.

Covenant Marriage vs. Contract Marriage

On August 15, 1997, the state of Louisiana put in place the nation's first modern covenant-marriage law. The law created a two-tier system of marriage. Couples could choose a *contract marriage*, with minimal formalities upfront and relative ease in attaining a no-fault divorce. Or they could choose a *covenant marriage*, with stringent policies governing the formation and dissolution of the marriage.

In Louisiana, and other states that have since adopted similar laws, those seeking a covenant marriage must receive detailed premarital instruction from a qualified religious official or professional counselor. In premarital counseling, both parties are advised that a covenant marriage is a lifelong commitment. Premarital counseling must also include a discussion of the seriousness of covenant marriage, the requirement to seek marriage counseling if marital difficulties develop, and the limited legal grounds available for ending the marriage by separation or divorce. Divorce under a covenant marriage is granted only for "serious fault" (such as adultery, capital felony, malicious desertion, or physical or sexual abuse).[1]

What Is a Covenant?

The term *covenant* appears 286 times in the Old Testament and twenty-four times in the New Testament. In ancient Israel, a covenant was very serious, solemn, and binding. When two people entered into a covenant, a goat or lamb would be slain and its carcass cut in half. With the two halves separated and placed on the ground, the two parties to the covenant ratified their agreement by walking between the two halves saying, "May God do so to me [that is, cut me in half] if I ever break this covenant with you and God."

A covenant requires both parties to uphold moral and legal faithfulness to the covenant for a lifetime, thereby uniting the individuals as one. Thus, when marriage was instituted by God with the words "they shall become one flesh," we can assume He was speaking of the covenant of marriage.

Malachi and the Covenant of Marriage

In Malachi, the final book of the Old Testament, God explains to Israel why He found their worship unacceptable. The people were distressed and weeping in frustration because God refused to accept their offerings, as evidenced by His withheld blessing. Through the prophet, He tells them that their worship is unacceptable because they have not been faithful to their marriage covenants.

> *You cover the altar of the LORD with tears, with weeping and crying; so He does not regard the offering anymore, nor receive it with goodwill from your hands. Yet you say, "For what reason?" Because the LORD has been witness between you and the wife of your youth, with whom you have dealt treacherously; yet she is your companion and your wife by covenant. But did He not make them one, having a remnant of the Spirit? And why one? He seeks godly offspring. Therefore take heed to your spirit, and let none deal treacherously with the wife of his youth. "For the LORD God of Israel says that He hates divorce, for it covers one's garment with violence," says the LORD of hosts. Therefore take heed to your spirit, that you do not deal treacherously.*
>
> MALACHI 2:13–16 NKJV

"Your wife by covenant." Malachi specifically identifies marriage as a covenant. A covenant in the Old Testament entailed a relationship with a non-relative that involved obligations and was established through an oath.

"The LORD has been witness between you and the wife of your youth." This statement reminds us that biblical marriage is not just a two-way *contract* between husband and wife. It is a *covenant*—a three-way

relationship in which the couple is accountable to God, for He bears witness to the agreement.

Because of the seriousness of the marriage covenant, spousal fidelity is inextricably linked to spiritual well-being. Elsewhere in scripture, we read that a marriage must be in good repair, or else the couple's prayers will be hindered (1 Peter 3:7; Matthew 5:23–34). Other passages speak of marriage as a covenant (see Genesis 2; Proverbs 2:17; Ezekiel 16:8–14), using covenantal language ("leave" and "hold fast") to describe a husband's duty. Also in Genesis 2, Adam commits himself to Eve, as God bears witness, by employing a covenant-ratifying formula: "This at last is bone of my bones and flesh of my flesh" (Genesis 2:23 ESV; see also 2 Samuel 5:1).

"You have dealt treacherously." This rebuke can be understood as, "You have broken your covenant marriage vows."

"Did He not make them [a man and his wife] one [flesh]?" Malachi speaks of covenant marriage partners as being "one." Malachi also emphasizes that *God* made marriage, not man. Therefore, man has no right to break it through divorce.

"[God] hates divorce." Divorce not only breaks the contract you made with your mate, it breaks the covenant you made with God. Therefore, God hates it.

"[Divorce] covers one's garment [a man's wife] with violence." God hates divorce because He sees it as the violent dismembering of a "one-flesh" covenant relationship. Marriage partners must "take heed" not to break the covenant they've made with each other and the Lord.

In covenant marriage, *two lives become one*. After being joined in the wedding ceremony, a husband and wife are thereafter identified with each other, and their two lives are supernaturally comingled. Finances are shared. Dreams are joined together. This coming together as one is signified through four symbolic acts:

1. *Establishment of a physical reminder of the promise*

When God entered a covenant with Noah to never again flood the earth, He gave Noah the rainbow as a testimony to His faithfulness (Genesis 9:16). Today, in a covenant marriage ceremony, the symbol of the promise is usually a ring, which serves as a constant reminder of the marriage bond.

2. *A change of name*

When God affirmed His covenant with Abram (which means "father"), He changed Abram's name to Abraham (meaning "father of many") and his wife's name from Sarai to Sarah (Genesis 17:5, 15). In covenant marriage, the wife takes her husband's name, symbolizing the *identity* and *oneness* that God intends for marriage partners.

3. *A shared meal*

Biblical covenants were often commemorated with a covenant meal. The most famous covenant meal is known as the Lord's Table or Communion, which Jesus hosted as He established the New Covenant on the night He was betrayed (1 Corinthians 11:24–25). In covenant marriage, couples may celebrate their new relationship by feeding each other wedding cake, which is a picture of sharing a common life and of two lives becoming one.

4. A witness is present

In the Old Testament, the solemnity of a covenant was often witnessed by setting up a memorial or sign. For example, when Jacob cut a covenant with his father-in-law, Laban, a heap of stones was set up to serve as a witness before God that neither party would break the covenant (Genesis 31:44–55). Similarly, when a man and a woman enter into the solemn, binding covenant of marriage, witnesses are present, the highest of which is God Himself.

Covenant vs. Contract

When I served as a pastor, I spent hours each week meeting with people about their marriages. I found that many of their struggles stemmed from a sense of frustration that one or both spouses had violated the contract. Many sought me out as a last resort to pressure their mate to fulfill the contract.

The tragedy is that so many couples today view marriage as merely a *contract*, not as a *covenant*. A *contract* is a business arrangement for the supply of goods or services at a fixed price. If the contract doesn't work out, the parties involved mutually agree to terminate the agreement and go their separate ways. Breaking a marriage contract through divorce has become easier and easier in the United States in the past several decades. In fact, *Time* ran an article as far back as 1993 stating that it was easier in the United States to walk away from a marriage than from a commitment to purchase a used car!

Christian marriage is not merely a social *contract* between *two* people. Biblical marriage is a sacred, lifelong *covenant* between *three* people—husband, wife, and God.

Covenant Marriages Are Stronger Marriages

God is perfectly wise and totally good. Therefore, when He established marriage as a covenant instead of a contract, He must have had good reasons for doing so. He must view covenant marriage as the wisest and best form of marriage.

One benefit of covenant marriage is *unconditional commitment*, a profoundly important factor in marital stability. God's intention for marriage is that both partners commit to absolute loyalty to the other person, the relationship as a whole, and the institution of marriage. Covenant marriage allows both husband and wife to thrive in an environment where they can say to each other, "I am unconditionally committed to love and be loved, to forgive and be forgiven, to serve and be served, and to know and be known."

A second benefit of covenant marriage is *sacrifice*. Spouses must be willing to live a life of sacrifice for the good of the other. In any number of life circumstances, they will be called upon to give more than an equal share. In contractual marriage, when tough times hit, partners are likely to walk out rather than sacrifice. In covenant marriage, walking out is not an option. Sacrifice is a choice one mate willingly makes for the other.

A third core characteristic of covenant marriage is *faithfulness* or *fidelity*. Breaking the marriage bond through adultery is not even a consideration. When temptation comes to be unfaithful, covenant partners renew their commitment to the marriage.

A fourth characteristic of covenant marriage is *security*. If you're confident that your mate is highly committed to you and your relationship; if you've seen evidence of his or her willingness to go the extra mile for you; and you know your spouse can be deeply trusted, then you can feel very secure.

Fifth, covenant marriage is *stronger* than contractual marriage. Instead of being an agreement between *two* people, it is a commitment between *three*. Ecclesiastes 4:12 says that "a three-fold cord is not quickly broken" (ESV). When you factor in that the third party in the covenant is *God*, you can be assured that the relationship is both strong and secure. What could be more empowering than having someone with a lifelong knowledge of your mate helping you? Or having the wisest person in the universe willing to give you advice. Or having all of His resources and connections available for your help.

Sixth, by fulfilling your covenant vows, you ultimately create the opportunity to find *deeper fulfillment* in marriage. In contractual marriage, couples often quit when the going gets tough. When that happens, they only experience the most superficial aspects of intimacy. But in covenantal marriage, a couple can't quit. They have to hang in there and work through the tough spots. If they do so wisely and well, they will inevitably break through too much deeper fulfillment than the relationship could have otherwise provided.

Covenant Marriages Challenge Us to Greater Growth

Gary Thomas, in his book *Sacred Marriage*, asks a significant question:

what if God designed marriage to make us holy more than to make us happy?[2] Thomas contends that "we can use the challenges, joys, struggles, and celebrations of marriage to draw closer to God and to grow in Christian character."[3] He recounts coming to a place of awareness that I have also experienced:

> I found that there was a tremendous amount of immaturity within me that my marriage directly confronted. The key was that I had to change my view of marriage. If the purpose of marriage was simply to enjoy an infatuation, and make me "happy," then I would need to get a "new" marriage every two to three years. But if I really wanted to see God transform me from the inside out, I'd need to concentrate on changing myself rather than on changing my spouse. In fact, you might say the more difficult my marriage proved to be, the more opportunity I'd have to grow.[4]

In contractual marriage, when the going gets tough, you can simply opt out by getting a divorce. But in covenant marriage, that option does not exist. Therefore, you have to dig down deep and desperately pursue God. That is when real growth—and, ultimately, deeper fulfillment—occurs in your marriage.

A Promise Kept

Robertson and Muriel McQuilkin served together as missionaries in Japan. Robertson later distinguished himself as president of Columbia International University. During this time, the vivacious Muriel became a sought-after speaker and hosted a popular radio show.

But that all changed when she was diagnosed with Alzheimer's. Gradually, she began to succumb to its ravages and was forced to abandon her radio show and speaking engagements. Initially, this was very hard on Robertson; but he had made a promise and taken vows to love and cherish her in sickness and in health. So he did.

As the disease took its toll on his wife, Robertson devoted more and more time to watching over her. When she became fearful and agitated in his absence, he left his job and other pursuits to care for her full time. Only when her husband was near was Muriel happy and content. Eventually, she became totally dependent on him, unable to perform rudimentary tasks or even converse.

It broke Robertson's heart to watch his lovely, intelligent wife slide into helpless dementia. But he remained with her gratefully and with a loving attitude. He reasoned that she had taken care of him for decades, and he found it a privilege to return the favor. He was not an angry or resentful caretaker. He saw his caretaking as a holy task, one entrusted to him by God.

Robertson McQuilkin's determination to fulfill his covenantal promise has been a blessing to thousands who have read his story.[5] More than that, it certainly has brought great pleasure and glory to God.

Notes
1. John Witte Jr. and Eliza Ellison, eds., *Covenant Marriage in Comparative Perspective* (Grand Rapids, MI: Eerdmans, 2005), 1.
2. Gary Thomas, *Sacred Marriage* (Grand Rapids, MI: Zondervan, 2007), 13.
3. Ibid., 12.
4. Ibid., 23.

5. You can read the McQuilkins' story in Robertson McQuilkin, *A Promise Kept* (Tyndale, 1998).

Chapter 3

Put God First

Every marriage has problems. As a counselor, I have seen the same scenario played out dozens of times: A distraught couple comes in for marriage counseling. After prayer, I ask them to tell me how they met and what type of marriage ceremony they had. Then I ask, "How can I help you?"

They begin to list all the problems in their marriage. (One wife reached into her purse and pulled out three pages of standard notebook paper, single spaced, listing the problems in her marriage and her husband's deficiencies!) I have heard couples list such sadly common (and correctible) complaints as these, among others:

He's not a spiritual leader.
All he does is beat me and the kids over
   the head with the Bible.
She's never interested in sex.
All he thinks about is sex.
He won't do anything around the house.
All she ever does is nag.
He puts his job ahead of the family.
She puts the kids ahead of our marriage.
I don't love him anymore.
I have no feelings for her anymore.

I have also heard couples tearfully recount much thornier issues:

Our daughter has special needs, and it is totally draining us.
Lately, it seems as if all we do is fight about money.
He lost his job three months ago. Now all he does is sulk. I
*   need him to step up and figure out how we can pay these bills.*
He says I'm too lenient with the kids, but I think he's too harsh.

And then there have been some really ugly issues, such as these:

She is having an affair with her boss.
He won't give up smoking pot.
She is depressed and drinking so much that she lost her
*   job. She doesn't do any housework, won't interact with the*
*   children, and hasn't gotten off the couch to fix a meal in weeks.*
He was under investigation by the IRS for tax fraud,
*   and then he was arrested last week because he was ccused*
*   of molesting my ten-year-old daughter.*

I learned a long time ago that other people's marital problems are beyond the scope of my control. I also learned that many issues go way beyond my expertise. So, instead of wading neck deep into their issues, I simply tell them, "If these are your only issues, then I have very good news for you today." That usually gets their attention. "There is great hope for your marriage," I continue. "God is still alive and sitting on the throne of the universe. And He is more committed to the success of your marriage than you are." Then I quote Matthew 19:

*"For this reason a man shall leave his father and mother and be joined to his wife, and the two shall become one flesh." So they are no longer two but one flesh. What therefore **God has joined together**, let no man separate.*

MATTHEW 19:5–6 NASB (EMPHASIS ADDED)

I tell the couple, "God joined you two together, and He is willing to help keep you together. I have seen God take situations that are worse than yours and rebuild a crumbling marriage into a strong one. So there is real hope for you today."

At this point, they are really listening. "I can guarantee you that God will do His part. But you both have to do your parts."

I can say the same to you as you read this book. No matter what issues your marriage is facing, God is committed to helping you. He has helped countless marriages in the past, and He will help yours. As we have said, marriage is a *three*fold covenant, and God takes His part in the covenant very seriously. Plus, He is the creator of marriage, the expert on marriage, and the smartest, wisest person in the universe. As long as God is still alive and on the throne, there is hope for your marriage.

Secret #3
Go to God.

Don't Leave God Out

Without the help of the LORD it is useless to build a home.

PSALM 127:1 CEV

In 1960, roughly 393,000 divorces occurred in the United States. By 1985, that number had tripled to 1,187,000. What happened? Among other factors, the Supreme Court voted in 1962 to legally "kick God out" of the public schools by removing school prayer. Under the misapplied notion of separation of church and state, the Ten Commandments were removed from classrooms, and Bible clubs were moved from campus or disbanded.

Children no longer started their day with God. They were educated in a secular system. When they got married, an increasing number did not start their marriages with God, build their marriages on God's Word, or turn to God when their marriages faced inevitable pressures and stresses. They did not consult His Word. They left God out. As a result, the "house" of their marriage crumbled.

Nearly every study of happy couples who have been married for a significant period of time reveals that one of the most important qualities of their marriages is "faith in God and spiritual commitment."[1] Building a marriage on God provides couples with a shared sense of values, ideology, and purpose that inevitably enhances their relationship.

Work the Triangle

Because marriage is a *three*-person covenant, and not merely a *two*-person contract, it can be represented as a triangle, with God at the top and the husband and wife on the other corners.

As Christians, our primary objective in life is to draw closer to God, as our Creator and Source. However, because of the triangular nature of marriage, note that as husbands and wives move up the sides of the triangle to get closer to God, they also end up getting closer to one another.

Pray Together and Enjoy Your Marriage More!

Dozens of surveys over the past twenty years have revealed the positive effect of vital Christianity on marital happiness. For example, one very recent survey found that couples who pray together "hold hands more often. . .make love more often. . .respect each other more, compliment more, and bicker less."[2]

Commenting on the findings of a 1989–1990 Gallup poll of marital happiness in America, author Andrew Greeley writes, "Religion is by far the most powerful correlate of marital attitudes and behavior. . . . Prayer, it is worth noting, is a much more powerful predictor of marital satisfaction than frequency of sexual intercourse."[3] Couples who prayed together and who went to church had significantly happier marriages.

Another study showed that "couples who frequently pray together are twice as likely as those who pray less often to describe their marriages as being highly romantic. They also report considerably higher sexual satisfaction and more sexual ecstasy!"[4]

Worship Together, Stay Together

Another recent survey concluded that for couples who attend church regularly, the divorce rate drops by 35 percent. Most tellingly, with a national divorce rate of one out of two marriages, of those couples who were married in a church, attended regularly, and prayed together as a couple, the divorce rate was only 1 out of 1,105![5]

Common sense tells us that couples who go to church and pray together are in close fellowship with other people who take their marriage vows seriously. They are more likely to get the emotional, social, and spiritual support they need from others. But they will especially be aided by God as they navigate the stresses and storms of married life.

Deepen Your Relationship with Your Mate by Deepening Your Relationship with God

In our over-busy, over-romanticized, self-centered, superficial culture, we too easily miss the obvious. Just as God fills and enhances our lives, He will fill and enrich our marriages, if we allow Him to. Les and Leslie Parrot unearthed an often overlooked aspect for building a better marriage:

> Superficiality is the curse of a restless marriage. The desperate need of most marriages is not for more excitement, more glitz, more activity. The soul of your marriage yearns for depth.[6]

As I develop my relationship with God, I find that He changes my perspective about everything, including marriage. Instead of looking for what I can get out of it, I am more interested in considering what I can add to it. I find I want to serve Cathy in order to bring greater glory to God. I have learned to look at my marriage as a fertile field for honoring God as I love, lead, serve, and pray for Cathy, even when I don't feel like it.

Serve Together

If both Cathy and I were to tell you about the best years of our marriage, they would correspond to the years we worked most closely together. During the first few years, while I finished seminary, we served together on weekends in a little church, doing visitation, leading children's church, directing the choir, and overseeing the youth ministry. It was a lot of hard work, usually fun; and best of all, it drew our marriage very close.

The next two years, I served as campus pastor for a Christian college, and Cathy worked with me several nights a week. We later started a new church and went visiting together three or four nights a week. Even when we weren't actually serving together, we had many shared experiences and relationships to talk about, laugh about, and pray about. Serving together has drawn our lives together, which has made us not only more effective teammates, but also better soul mates.

Run to God. . .on Your Knees

God takes His part in the threefold covenant of marriage very seriously. No matter what marriage issues we face, God is committed to help us. He promises that, if we will come to Him, He will give us the grace we need.

> *Let us draw near with confidence to the throne of grace,*
> *so that we may receive mercy and find grace to help in time of need.*
> HEBREWS 4:16 NASB

When Jesus ascended into heaven after His resurrection from the dead, He did not leave us to fend for ourselves. He sent God the Holy Spirit to help us (John 14:16; 16:7).

One way the Holy Spirit supports us is by helping us pray. He crafts the words and requests *in us* that reflect our real desires as well as God's. Beyond that, when we are so overwhelmed that we have no idea what to pray, the Holy Spirit intercedes *for us*.

> *In the same way the Spirit also helps our weakness;*
> *for we do not know how to pray as we should, but the Spirit*
> *Himself intercedes for us with groanings too deep for words. . .*
> *because He intercedes for the saints according to the will of God.*
> ROMANS 8:26–27 NASB

One of the best things I have done through the years is pray about what to pray about. Let me explain. I ask the Lord to show me what I need to pray about for my wife and for our marriage. Typically, after I've prayed this way for several days, a verse or phrase will come to mind that perfectly fits our present situation. I then incorporate this verse or phrase into my prayers for the next three or four months. During that time, I can see God at work.

For example, about ten years ago, Cathy and I were not on the same page at all. Her life was wrapped up in the kids, and mine was in the church. We were not taking time for our relationship. I was away for a few days at a conference in Colorado when God spoke to me about my need to pray for Cathy and our marriage.

I told the Lord that Cathy and I were heading in such different directions that I did not even know what to pray. Over the next two days, He answered quite clearly. In my personal Bible reading, I happened to be in Matthew and read these words:

> *"The two shall become one flesh."*
> *So they are no longer two but one.*
> MATTHEW 19:5–6 ESV

The words *one flesh* jumped out at me as if they were in bold print. So did the phrase "they are no longer two but one."

The next day, during a prayer time at the conference, one of the men asked what he should pray about for me. All I told him was, "Please pray for my marriage."

He began to pray these words: "Lord, I sense that Dave and Cathy are walking down two separate paths right now. Please put them together on one path—Your path. May they hike through life together as one."

Okay, Lord, I thought. *I get it. I need to pray that Cathy and I will truly be "one flesh." I also ask You to show me how to make that happen.*

After I got home, I began to pray every day that Cathy and I would be on the same path at the same time. One day I was talking with a man who had been hiking on the Appalachian Trail. As we talked, the thought hit me, *That's it! Cathy and both love to hike. This year we should go away for our anniversary and hike on the Appalachian Trail.*

Over the next few years, we hiked the Appalachian Trail for our anniversary. After hiking all day, we stayed at a nice bed-and-breakfast each night.

We both loved it. But the best part was that, as we hiked, we had time to talk on a level that we hadn't since the boys were born. Soon we were back on the same page, on the same path, together as one.

Jesus Is Praying for Your Marriage. . .Right Now!

Sometimes it feels overwhelming to try to make a marriage work in the midst of all the other stresses, pressures, troubles, and heartaches of life. Remember, you are not alone. God the Father is committed to help your marriage, and Jesus continually prays for your marriage. Stop for a moment and read those last six words again, slowly: *Jesus continually prays for your marriage.*

> *Therefore He is able also to save to the uttermost (completely, perfectly, finally, and for all time and eternity) those who come to God through Him, since He is always living to make petition to God and intercede with Him and intervene for them.*
> HEBREWS 7:25 AMP

Wow! Be encouraged. Right this moment, Jesus is addressing the Father on your behalf, and on behalf of your mate and your marriage. Jesus is praying for *your* marriage. . .right now!

Notes

1. D. L. Fennell, "Characteristics of Long-Term Marriages," *Journal of Mental Health Counseling*, 15 (1993): 446–60.

2. Quoted in the *Fort Worth Star-Telegram*, "Praying Together Means More Than Just Staying Together, Authors Say," February 14, 2008.

3. Andrew Greeley, *Faithful Attraction: Discovering Intimacy, Love and Fidelity in American Marriage* (New York: Tor, 1991), 221, 230.

4. Les and Leslie Parrot, *Saving Your Marriage Before It Starts: Seven Questions to Ask Before and After You Marry* (Grand Rapids, MI: Zondervan, 1995), 150.

5. This statistic is quoted in Building a Foundation for the Family, an audio series by Dr. John C. Maxwell (Injoy, 1992).

6. Parrot, *Saving Your Marriage*, 147.

Chapter 4

Celebrate Your Differences

W hat on earth is going on? I think I'm on fire!"
It was three o'clock in the morning on a cold winter night, and I was physically burning up. Sweat soaked my side of the sheets. I like to sleep a little cool, and I was anything but cool. Cathy heard me stirring and rolled over.

"I'm freezing!" she said. "This electric blanket just does not seem to be working. Even though I keep turning it up, I keep getting colder."

"The controls must be broken," I added knowingly. "I keep turning it down and am only getting hotter."

It was a brand-new electric blanket. We had gotten it as a wedding gift for our first winter together, and we were excited because it had dual controls. Cathy could be as warm as she wanted, and I could be as cool as I wanted.

Of course, the blanket and the controls worked just fine. We simply had the blanket and the controls backwards. Cathy had the controls for my half of the bed and I had the controls for hers. When she turned it up, it made my side warmer. When I turned it down, it made her side colder.

I am embarrassed to admit that we slept in misery for several nights before we figured it out. But once we got the controls right, the blanket worked just great. Cathy could turn it up and be warm. I could turn it down and be cool. The dual controls facilitated our differences effectively.

When God created marriage, He intentionally designed it to be the joining of two distinct genders. Man needed a corresponding complement. He did not need someone exactly like him (like another man), but someone like him in many ways, yet different in several ways as well. He needed a suitable companion. So God created woman from man.

But for Adam no suitable helper was found. So the LORD God caused the man to fall into a deep sleep; and while he was sleeping, he took one of the man's ribs and then closed up the place with flesh. Then the LORD God made a woman from the rib he had taken out of the man, and he brought her to the man.

The man said, "This is now bone of my bones and flesh of my flesh; she shall be called 'woman,' for she was taken out of man." That is why a man leaves his father and mother and is united to his wife, and they become one flesh.

GENESIS 2:20–24 NIV

The immediate joy and challenge of marriage is for two separate individuals to learn to complement each other and unite together in order to become one flesh. From the account in Genesis, several applicable truths are evident:

1. Men and women are different.
2. The differences exist in order to make the whole stronger than the sum of its parts.
3. The differences are what make the opposite sex so attractive— and so frustrating.

4. The challenge of uniting two very different people is what drives us to God to see Him do the mysterious and glorious work of making us one.

5. Marriages are enhanced as we understand, appreciate, and use our differences to complement one another and draw close, not criticize each other and draw away.

Secret #4

Understand your mate and celebrate your differences.

Viva la Différence!

Men and women are different. Someone has said that the world would have a lot better marriages if men tried to understand their wives and wives tried to understand football. At any rate, wise marriage partners learn to celebrate and cooperate with their differences.

Different Tendencies

Not long after we were married, I began to see how different Cathy and I are. We were playing Monopoly with her parents, and I failed to realize that Cathy's goal was for us to get to know each other better, have fun, and all get along. My goal was to bankrupt her parents (in the game!) and wipe them off the board, swiftly and completely. Cathy could not believe how "insensitive and aggressive" I was. I could not believe she was upset with me for winning. Why else do you play a game?

God created men and women to have different tendencies, emotionally, romantically, and intuitively.

Women tend to be more emotion based, and men are usually more reason based. Women lean toward being more sensitive. They feel things more readily. They are more subjective. They may cry more than men, but often they are unable to verbalize why they are crying. On the other hand, men are usually more fact oriented. They are more logical and objective. Unfortunately, this often makes them less sensitive.

Women tend to emphasize relationships with people. Men focus on projects. For example, if a couple attends a baseball game, the husband is more likely to keep score, and the wife is more likely to watch people. Women are wonderful at focusing on the necessary responsibilities at hand. Men focus on the larger challenges and objectives.

Women tend to identify easily. Men are more emotionally detached. For example, if they are watching a football game and one of the players on the opposing team is injured, the wife will gasp and wonder what the player's wife is feeling. Meanwhile, her husband will be yelling for the trainers to get the injured player off the field so the game can continue.

Women tend to be more verbally expressive than men. Men are more physically expressive. The average woman uses about twenty-five thousand words a day. The average man uses about ten thousand. A mom will tell her kids she loves them. The father will wrestle with them on the living room floor.

Women usually respond to attention, men to admiration. Many a woman's entire day can be made or lost based on how her hair looks and whether she feels as if she looks okay in her outfit. Most men, if they closed their eyes, probably couldn't even tell you what they had on.

Especially at the beginning of marriage, women are more home and family–centered than men. Men are much more focused on their careers and hobbies. For example, when women get together, they talk about their children, their husbands, their parents, and their friends. Men talk about their jobs and sports, or hunting and fishing.

Romantically, women tend to be more responsive to words and touch, whereas men are more responsive to visual cues. This explains why many more men than women are addicted to pornography. Women are primarily attracted to a man based on his personality. Men are initially attracted to a woman based on her looks. This explains why models often marry homely comedians or musicians, and why men are attracted to models and actresses.

Women tend to have keener intuition than men. They often read subliminal messages quickly. They tend to work through a decision based on how it feels. They often can evaluate a person's character quickly (and seemingly mysteriously, to many men). Men, on the other hand, reason through decisions by weighing out various factors and combining intuition and reason.

It's important to realize, however, that these differing tendencies are not necessarily right or wrong. They are just different. Strong marriages and families are built when both spouses are directed by the Holy Spirit and work in understanding and cooperation with one another.

Different Responses

Because God assigned husbands a leadership role in marriage, He designed wives to subconsciously react to the effectiveness or ineffectiveness of their husbands' leadership. A wife tends to react to the signals her husband sends and the circumstances he creates. As I began to understand this, I realized that if I was not happy with my wife's responses, I should look in the mirror for the cause. Often she was simply reacting to my actions, or lack thereof.

Gary Smalley analyzes and summarizes this tendency in his helpful book *If Only She Knew*. Look through the chart and see where these situations are being played out in your marriage.

As you can see, this cause-and-effect relationship can easily become a negative cycle. For example, if the wife feels as if her husband is inattentive, her response may be to become domineering. As someone once noted, when she doesn't feel like a queen, she starts building a castle. Often, though, this response only makes him more inattentive—which makes her even more domineering.

These tendencies can also create a positive cycle. For example, I found that if I was less lazy or distracted and did a better job of taking care of things around the house as soon as Cathy brought them to my attention—or, even better, *before* she noticed them—then she didn't nag me.

Obviously, both the husband and the wife are responsible before God for their own actions and reactions. Your mate's behavior is never an excuse for your sin. Also, you can make it much easier for your mate to act or react positively if you act or react positively first.

We cannot control the other person's attitudes or behavior. We can only control our own. I've observed that, ninety-nine times out of a hundred, when a husband works on his actions, it positively affects his wife's reactions.

Different Responsibilities

God has given wives and husbands different responsibilities. The chart below summarizes the differences.

Different Love Languages

In many ways, love is as much a language as Spanish or Chinese. Many marriages flounder because the spouses fail to understand and speak their mate's language of love. Communication and intimacy can be as severely limited as if you insisted on speaking Spanish even though your mate only understood Chinese. If you want your mate to feel loved, learn to speak his or her love language.

Though others later popularized the concept, Judson Swihart identified eight languages of love in his 1977 classic, *How Do You Say "I Love You"?* As you look through the following list, note the ways in which you *feel* and *express* love, and the ways in which your spouse receives and expresses love.

The Eight Languages of Love

Say it with words.
Say it with touch.
Say it with time together.
Say it with helping out.
Say it with material things.
Say it with loyalty.
Say it with meeting emotional needs.
Say it with bringing out the best and challenging.

Everyone is different. God has given each of us a unique personality. If we don't understand our own personality, as well as our mate's, we will needlessly irritate and annoy each other. But if we understand and appreciate our personality and our mate's, we will find that God has wisely put us together to strengthen one another and work together most effectively.

Perhaps the most common way of discussing and understanding common personalities is through the lens of four personality types. As best we can tell, this way of understanding personality goes back before the time of Christ to a man named Hippocrates.

Hippocrates was an ancient Greek physician (c. 460–370 BC) who has been referred to as "the father of medicine." He has been credited as the author of the Hippocratic Oath, a document on the ethics of medical practice. Hippocrates believed that certain human behaviors could be understood and related to the classical elements of air, water, earth, and fire. These are commonly referred to as the four temperaments: sanguine, phlegmatic, melancholic, and choleric, respectively.

As time progressed, numerous other paradigms were devised, which measured not only temperament but also various individual aspects of personality and behavior. Perhaps the most commonly used model is a four-quadrant system called DISC, based on the work of psychologist William Moulton Marston. DISC, which stands for Dominance, Influence, Steadiness, and Conscientiousness, examines the behavior of individuals within a specified environment.[1] DISC looks at behavioral styles and preferences. Examine the charts below and place a check mark by the characteristics that are most true of you. Try to pick only one per row. When you are finished, add up each column. Are you more of a D, I, S, or C? What about your mate?

D	I	S	C
Dominance	Influence	Steadiness	Conscientiousnes s
Aggressive	Talkative	Security	Cautiousness
Will power	Emotional	Unemotional	Perfectionist
Control and power	People and social situations	Patience and persistence	Rules and structure
Assertiveness	Communication	Thoughtfulness	Organization
Extroverted	Extroverted	Introverted	Introverted
Paul	Peter	Abraham	Moses
Lion	Otter	Golden Retriever	Beaver
Bear	Monkey	Dolphin	Owl
Intimidator	Poor Me	Aloof	Interrogator
Salsa	Swing Dance	Waltz	Tango
Total:	Total:	Total:	Total:

Put a check mark by every characteristic that is usually true regarding your personality.

D	I	S	C
Demanding	Expressive	Solid	Analytical
Choleric	Sanguine	Phlegmatic	Melancholy
Direct	Spirited	Considerate	Systematic

Powerful	Popular	Peaceful	Perfect
Self-propelled	Spirited	Solid	Systematic
Administrative	Active	Amiable	Analytical
Leader	Expresser	Dependable	Analyst
Production	Connection	Status Quo	Harmony
Driven	Influencing	Steadiness	Cautiousness/ Compliance
Common Sense	Dynamic	Innovative	Analytic
Total:	Total:	Total:	Total:

Put a check mark by the characteristic most often true of you.

D	I	S	C
Directing	Communicative	Amiable	Analytic
Guardian	Artisan	Philosopher	Scientist
Motivated	Messy	Casual	Compulsive
Controller	Promoter	Supporter	Analyst
Mastery	Belonging	Generosity	Independence
Achiever	Attached	Altruistic	Autonomous
Power	Significance	Virtue	Competence
Adventurer	Helper	Peacemaker	Asserter
Achiever	Romantic	Observer	Perfectionist
Total:	Total:	Total:	Total:

Now total up the findings from the three charts.

D	I	S	C
Chart one:	Chart one:	Chart one:	Chart one:
Chart two:	Chart two:	Chart two:	Chart two:
Chart three:	Chart three:	Chart three:	Chart three:
Total:	Total:	Total:	Total:

Which column is highest for you? D, I, S, or C?

What is your primary personality type?

How has God wired your mate?

How does your primary personality type affect the way you relate to your mate?

Cathy and I have the same set of values but different personalities. I am a high D. Cathy is a high I. We both love God. We both love each other. Many of the fights we endured in our early years of marriage were basically the result of misunderstanding the other's God-given personality. Now we have learned that when we make the effort to understand and work with the other's personality, everything is very, very good. When we don't make the effort. . .well. . .things don't work out quite so well.

Putting It All Together

Read back through this chapter with your mate. Share honestly about yourself. As your mate shares, listen openly, with a teachable attitude, seeking to better understand your mate so you can love him or her more effectively.

Discuss which male and female tendencies you note in your
marriage and discuss what you can do to better complement
them.

Go through the section on responses and discuss what the
husband does or does not do and how the wife tends to react.

Talk about your God-given responsibilities and how you
both are living them out in your marriage.

Read through the eight love languages and discuss each
other's primary language(s).

5. Share your findings from the temperament assessment
and talk through how your different temperaments affect
your relationship.

Celebrate!

Remember, it was probably your differences that first attracted you to
your mate. Wise marriage partners understand and appreciate their
differences. Learn to use your differences to complement rather than
criticize your mate. Use them to draw closer to each other instead of
drawing a way. See God's wisdom in putting you together with your
spouse, and cooperate with God to deepen your love through, and
because of, your differences.

Notes
1. William Moulton Marston, *Emotions of Normal People* (New York:
Harcourt, Brace, 1928).

Chapter 5

Love and Respect

What would you say if I told you that you could greatly reduce the number of conflicts you and your mate will experience in your marriage?

Would you like to know how to act toward your spouse so as to energize your marriage and enhance your intimacy?

Are you interested in learning a cycle of behavior that will either make or break your marriage?

Would you believe me if I told you that the big secret to a better marriage has been readily available for two thousand years, but that few couples know it and even fewer apply it?

What does every wife long for from her husband and every husband need from his wife? The apostle Paul, writing under divine inspiration, shared the secret most clearly in his letter to the Ephesians.

> *Husbands, love your wives as Christ loved the church and gave himself up for her. . . . However, let each one of you love his wife as himself, and let the wife see that she respects her husband.*
> EPHESIANS 5:25, 33 ESV

Did you catch it? Husbands are to give their wives *love*, and wives are to show their husbands *respect*. Wise couples never underestimate the power of unconditional love and respect.

Secret #5
Husband, unconditionally love your wife.
Wife, unconditionally respect
your husband.

God Knows

Remember, God not only created marriage, He also created men and women. He knows that men need unconditional respect. He also knows that women have a primary need for unconditional love. He needs admiration. She needs attention. He needs approval. She needs affection.

Therefore, when God tells a husband to love his wife, it's because He knows that love is what she needs. Likewise, when God tells a wife to respect her husband, it's because He knows that respect is exactly what the husband needs from his wife.

Not surprisingly, scientific research confirms the power of love and respect. Dr. John Gottman, a professor at the University of Washington, spent twenty years studying two thousand couples who had been married between twenty and forty years to the same mate. These diverse couples had one common denominator—the loving, respectful tone of their conversations. Gottman observed "a strong undercurrent of two basic ingredients: love and respect."[1]

Unconditional Love and Respect

As we will discuss in detail in the next chapter, a husband's love for his wife is to be patterned after Christ's unconditional love for His church. Similarly, as we will see in the remainder of this chapter, a wife's respect for her husband also is to be without limits (Ephesians 5:22–24; 1 Peter 3:1–6).

It should be noted that Paul's admonition is more than just a really smart suggestion. It is an imperative that must be followed. That means a husband is to love his wife *even if* she does not obey the command to respect him; and the wife is to respect her husband *even if* he does not obey the command to love her. In other words, spouses cannot condition their own obedience on the obedience of the other. Husbands must love and wives must respect—*unconditionally*. Furthermore, the command for a husband to love his wife does not mean that he loves her only *in proportion* to how much she respects him. Neither should the wife respect her husband only in proportion to how much he loves her.

The commands to love and respect are not contingent upon how the mate is holding up his or her end of the deal. It is a matter of obedience. Disobedience is not an option.

Spiral Up or Spiral Down

I have sat in dozens of counseling sessions, listening to couples express very real and deep frustrations. When they finish with their litany, I am able to give them some good news: God gave every married couple the key to turn their marriage around and head in the right direction. He gave the commands to love and respect for good reason.

If the husband will love and the wife will respect, the marriage will begin to spiral upward. No matter where a couple starts, their marriage can go as high as they both wish, *if* both will diligently and consistently do their part. The more they put into it, the faster their marriage will climb. This spiral also has a negative side, which Emerson Eggerichs calls the Crazy Cycle: "Without love from him, she reacts without respect; without respect from her, he reacts without love."[2] In other words, if the husband fails to love and the wife fails to respect, the marriage spirals downward. The less love and respect, the faster the downward descent.

You Can Speed the Process

The beautiful aspect of the love and respect spiral is that you have the power to speed the process. The more the husband gives his wife love, the easier it will be for her to respect him. In the same way, the more the wife respects her husband, the easier it will be for him to love her.

Wives, if you want more love, show more respect. Unconditional respect is as powerful for your husband as unconditional love is for you.

Husbands, if you want more respect, show more love. Unconditional love is as powerful for your wife as unconditional respect is for you.

Just as you can accelerate the process, you can also slow it down or even send it in the wrong direction. If a wife does not receive love from her husband, she will not give respect in return. And if he doesn't feel respected, her husband will react without love.

Men Need Respect

"Respect" is a song written and originally released by recording artist Otis Redding in 1965. In 1967 it became a hit and the signature song of R&B singer Aretha Franklin. It was inducted into the Grammy Hall of Fame in 1998. In 2002 the Library of Congress honored Franklin's version by adding it to the National Recording Registry. It is number five on

Rolling Stone's list of "The 500 Greatest Songs of All Time." I am sure you're familiar with the refrain:

R-E-S-P-E-C-T
Find out what it means to me. . .
All I'm askin' is for a little respect. . .
I got to have (just a little bit)
A little respect (just a little bit)
R-E-S-P-E-C-T

The overwhelming response to the song is obviously an indication of the need for and importance of honor in a marriage relationship. Honoring others has become a forgotten virtue in our culture and in too many of our marriages. Yet it is a vital aspect of love and an absolute essential for a strong marriage.

Even though a woman made the song famous, it was written by a man. Wise wives understand that respect is a man's deepest need (just a little bit).

In a national study, four hundred men were asked to choose between two uniquely negative scenarios:

A. Being left alone and unloved in the world, or
B. Feeling inadequate and disrespected by everyone

Seventy-four percent said that if they had to choose one, they would choose to be alone and unloved. Most men do not want to feel inadequate or disrespected.[3] Although it is very difficult for women to understand, most men would rather be in a marriage where they are deeply respected but not loved than be in a marriage where they are loved but not respected.

Nothing motivates a husband to give his wife genuine love and spiritual leadership like feeling trusted, admired, honored, and respected by her. On the other hand, nothing de-motivates a husband to try to love and lead his wife as much as feeling dishonored, disrespected, and distrusted by her.

Wives Need to Show Respect

Paul is very clear about the wife's responsibility to show respect to her husband. In the book of Colossians, he tells wives to show respect by practicing submission.

> *Wives, submit to your husbands, as is fitting in the Lord.*
>
> COLOSSIANS 3:18 ESV

In his letter to the Ephesians, Paul went into more detail. He compares the necessary submission of the wife to her husband with the vital submission of the church to Christ. Notice that she is to submit "in everything."

> *Wives, submit to your own husbands, as to the Lord. For the husband is the head of the wife even as Christ is the head of the church, his body, and is himself its Savior. Now as the church submits to Christ, so also wives should submit in everything to their husbands.*
>
> EPHESIANS 5:22–24 ESV

I have often had wives ask me, "But doesn't my husband first need to earn my respect?" The answer is. . .no. There is no verse in the Bible that says the husband must first earn his wife's respect before she is obligated to give it. *Unconditional* respect means just that. She is to respect him whether or not he has met the conditions of deserving it.

I am also asked by wives, "At what point am I no longer obligated to submit to my husband? Is it when I don't like the direction he is taking? Is it when he is making a bad decision?" I understand their point. Often the wife is the more competent decision maker. Often husbands don't seek God for direction before making decisions. But Paul said, "Submit *in everything*." In my opinion, the only thing that could trump "in everything" would be if the husband were ordering the wife to do something that was clearly immoral, illegal, or unbiblical.

Of course, no wife wants to be a doormat to a domineering, overbearing husband. She also does not want to be a hypocrite, giving respect when she does not feel it. Further, she does not want to feel trapped in an unloving marriage. God knew that when He had Paul write, "Wives, submit to your own husbands *as to the Lord*" (Ephesians 5:22 ESV, emphasis added). The wife's submission is to be a way in which she serves and trusts the Lord. Her submission is a spiritual issue. It involves trusting the Lord to lead her through her imperfect husband.

It takes faith.

It is also very effective.

Paul wasn't the only one addressing the wife's need to respect her husband. Consider the apostle Peter's divinely inspired advice to wives:

> *In the same way, you wives, be submissive to your own husbands*
> *so that even if any of them are disobedient to the word,*
> *they may be won without a word by the behavior of their*

wives, as they observe your chaste and respectful behavior.

1 Peter 3:1–2 NASB

Here Peter tells wives to submit to their husbands "even if" the husbands are carnal or unbelieving! Why? So that they may be won over—not by the wife's continual arguing and nagging, but instead by her silence and her respectful behavior.

Peter says that if the wife wants the cycle of love and respect to spiral upward so that she is given more love, she can make that happen by giving her husband respect.

Your adornment must not be merely external—braiding the hair, and wearing gold jewelry, or putting on dresses; but let it be the hidden person of the heart, with the imperishable quality of a gentle and quiet spirit, which is precious in the sight of God. For in this way in former times the holy women also, who hoped in God, used to adorn themselves, being submissive to their own husbands; just as Sarah obeyed Abraham, calling him lord, and you have become her children if you do what is right without being frightened by any fear.

1 Peter 3:3–6 NASB

The wife must respect her husband.

Ephesians 5:33 NIV

Win the Battle, Lose the War

Every marriage counselor has seen it time and again. Too often the wife is guilty of trying to win battles, but she ends up losing the war. She gets into a pattern of approaching her husband with nagging, reminding, correcting, arguing, and manipulating with anger, in order to get him to not work late, to spend more time with the kids, to not forget things, and to do more around the house. Yet she loses the war, because instead of inspiring him to love her more, these little tactics only drive him to love her less. They make him feel disrespected and they shut off his heart.

No husband wants to feel as if his wife's goal in life is to fix him, train him, or change him. No husband wants to be corrected, instructed, nagged, yelled at, or mothered into submission to his wife.

Wise wives stop trying to fix, train, or change their husbands. Instead they show them respect.

R-E-S-P-E-C-T

"Okay, I see what the Bible says about respecting my husband," a wife sincerely asked me. "But how do I do it? Could you spell it out for me?"

I took the acrostic R-E-S-P-E-C-T and combined it with a husband's deepest needs. She was wise enough to do the rest.

R: *Recognize his God-given desire to work and achieve.* God made your husband to be as passionate about his job as you are passionate about the children. Support his attempts to do well.

E: *Esteem highly his God-given need to protect and provide.* Never devalue his income or efforts to provide for you and your family.

S: *Salute his attempts to show spiritual leadership in your marriage, family, and church.* Let him make the call and learn to trust God for the results. Realize that he will not always do it your way, but that may be a good thing.

P: *Provide for his need for sexual fulfillment.* Accept the fact that his sexual needs are different from yours. As long as his needs aren't fully met, it will be very difficult for him to meet your emotional needs for love.

E: *Eliminate nagging, reminding, correcting, arguing, and manipulating with anger.* These tactics will only close his heart.

C: *Connect with him as a friend and a recreational companion.* Men are energized by and communicate through shared experiences, more than by talking about them.

T: *Thank God for your husband, and thank your husband for his attempts to show you love.* Every man wants to see himself as a great lover, even though he is not. If he feels that his efforts are appreciated, he will be motivated to try more often.

Be Her Hero

A wise husband will make it easy for his wife to respect him and for God to convict her when she is not. How? The answer is simple: be the type of man your wife can respect and admire. If that does not sound very compelling, allow me to use a word that might resonate more with you: *hero*. Be your wife's hero.

No woman is inspired by a spiritual wimp.

No wife deserves to be stuck with a selfish slob.

No little girl dreams of marrying a couch potato.

No little boy grows up dreaming of being just "a nice guy."

Nine times out of ten, if the husband will step up and truly lead, serve, and love his wife, she will respond with genuine respect. She will actively admire his hard work, his wise counsel, his courage of convictions, firm faith, solid priorities, and gentle love.

Paul summarizes a target for husbands at the end of his letter to the Corinthians.

> *Be alert and on your guard; stand firm in your faith (your conviction respecting man's relationship to God and divine things, keeping the trust and holy fervor born of faith and a part of it). Act like men and be courageous; grow in strength! Let everything you do be done in love (true love to God and man as inspired by God's love for us).*
>
> 1 CORINTHIANS 16:13–14 AMP

You Can Do It

Maybe it seems overwhelming to consider giving your mate the unconditional *respect* that God demands. Realize that if God commands you to do it, He is obligated to enable you to fulfill His command. Ask God to help you do your part to meet your mate's deepest needs.

Notes

1. John Gottman, *Why Marriages Succeed or Fail* (New York: Simon & Schuster, 1994), 61.
2. Emerson Eggerichs, *Love and Respect* (Brentwood, TN: Integrity Publishing, 2004), 6.
3. This survey was conducted by Decision Analyst, Inc., on behalf of author Shaunti Feldhahn. See Shaunti Feldhahn, *For Women Only: What you Need to Know about the Inner Lives of Men* (Portland, OR: Multnomah, 2004).

Chapter 6

Meet Your Mate's Needs

When Dan and Tina came in for marriage counseling, I could tell it was going to be one of those days.

After the preliminaries, I asked, "Tina, what would you say is the biggest problem in this marriage?"

"Pastor Dave," she began, "I can't take being in a loveless marriage any longer."

"Are you saying that Dan does not love you?"

"Yes," she said as she started to cry.

"Dan, do you love Tina?"

"Yes. If I didn't, I wouldn't be here."

"Tina, please tell us *why* you say that Dan does not love you."

Tina wiped her eyes with a handkerchief and opened her purse. She reached in and pulled out a neatly folded list, which she proceeded to read:

1. *We can barely pay our bills, but then Dan goes out and buys a new hunting rifle without even talking to me about it.*
2. *Dan has no interest in me or our children. If the subject is not some dumb animal in a field that he can shoot at, or something on TV, or one of his projects in the garage, he could care less about it.*
3. *Dan never really talks to me anymore. He just talks* at *me or grunts on his way to watch TV. He used to open up and share how he felt, but that stopped after we got married.*

4. The only time Dan ever touches me is when he wants sex.

5. Dan never helps with anything around the house. I have to work all day, come home, clean the house, fix the meals, and tend to the children all by myself. If I am going to have to do it all myself anyway, I would rather do it without having to clean up after him.

6. Dan obviously does not love me.

Later that afternoon, I received a phone call from another distraught wife.

"Dave, I don't know what to do." It was Ashley, one of our neighbors, on the other line. "Josh says he wants a divorce."

"Okay," I said slowly. "What else did he say?"

"He said that he doesn't love me anymore. I don't meet his needs. . .and. . .he has found someone else. Would you try to talk to him?"

So I called Josh and said, "Josh, Ashley told me that you want a divorce. What's going on?"

"Look, Dave, I know you are trying to help, but I just don't love her anymore. I haven't felt anything for her in several years."

"But, Josh, you know that love is more than a feeling. Love is a commitment."

"Well, she obviously doesn't love me," Josh snapped.

"What makes you say that?"

"Look, Ashley's a nice person to everyone else, but not to me. She *says* she loves me, but it is obvious that she doesn't even *like* me."

"What makes you say that?"

Josh was ready with his answer. "After we had been married only a few weeks, I realized that her great goal in life was to change me or fix me. In her mind, I never do anything right. I am respected by everyone at work, but when I come home she treats me like I am an idiot. She belittles or questions every decision I make. Plus, she expects me to read her mind. And if I happen to guess wrong—watch out. She yells at me. Then, if I try to defend myself, she either blows up or she cries and calls me insensitive."

"Josh," I said, when he took a breath, "Ashley told me there was another woman involved."

"That is a very recent development," he replied. "But I have been feeling this way for some time. As you know, Ashley has gained over sixty pounds since we got married. Plus, she never seems interested in sex. We only have sex a couple times a month, and then she acts like she's doing me a big favor. Look, I'm not asking for sex every night, but I do have needs, and she obviously is not interested in meeting them. My mind is made up. Good-bye."

With that, he hung up the phone.

Although both marriages were undergoing different problems, the core issues were very similar. Josh wanted a divorce because he felt that Ashley wasn't meeting his needs. Tina wanted a divorce because she felt that Dan wasn't meeting her needs.

Secret #6
Understand your mate's needs,
and try to meet them.

Though I am familiar with several authors who discuss the notion of "relational banking," the apostle Paul also mentions this concept in his second letter to the Corinthians. Notice that he describes his love in terms of spending and being spent.

> *And I will very gladly spend and be spent for your souls;*
> *though the more abundantly I love you, the less I am loved.*
>
> 2 CORINTHIANS 12:15 NKJV

In reference to marriage, psychologist Willard Harley does a great job of describing the love bank:

I believe each of us has a Love Bank. It contains many different accounts, one for each person we know. Each person either makes deposits or withdrawals whenever we interact with him or her. Pleasurable interactions cause deposits, and painful interactions cause withdrawals.[1]

When a spouse's love bank account is full, through many or large positive deposits, he or she feels loved. If the account is depleted, through many or sizable withdraws, he or she will feel unloved.

Often the mate with unmet needs will be tempted to look elsewhere to have those needs met. Harley contends that marriages do not fail through incompatibility as much as from depleted love banks.[2] The way to help your mate feel loved is by making deposits. Deposits are made through meeting your spouse's basic and intimate relational needs.

Love is expressed by seeing a need *and* extending yourself to meet it.

> *If anyone has material possessions and sees a brother or sister in need*
> *but has no pity on them, how can the love of God be in that person? Dear*
> *children, let us not love with words or speech but with actions and in truth.*
> 1 JOHN 3:17–18 NIV

> *Suppose a brother or a sister is without clothes and daily food.*
> *If one of you says to them, "Go in peace; keep warm and well fed,"*
> *but does nothing about their physical needs, what good is it?*
> JAMES 2:15–16 NIV

In marriage, we make a pledge to love our spouse. Marriage is a unique relationship, in that two people commit themselves exclusively to meet certain intense and intimate needs in each other. Each mate gives the other the exclusive right to meet those specific needs, and also agrees not to allow anyone else to meet those needs.

This mutual restriction and dependence is one thing that makes marriage beautiful, sacred, and fulfilling. When our needs are met in marriage, we experience intense pleasure and growing love. But when our needs are neglected, deep resentment and frustration arise. Frustration makes the mate with unmet needs a more likely candidate for adultery. He or she may begin to look outside the marriage to have those needs met.

A wise mate seeks to discover, understand, and fulfill the unique relational needs that only he or she can adequately and honorably meet. Doing so wonderfully enhances the marriage.

As we discussed in the previous chapter, the husband's primary need from his wife is respect. Emerson Eggerichs writes, "Husbands are made to be respected, want respect, and expect to be respected."[3] A husband's love bank is filled when he feels respected by his wife.

Willard Harley states that, after counseling thousands of couples with troubled marriages, he is able to list the basic needs of husbands and wives. He says that a man's five most basic needs in marriage tend to be (1) sexual fulfillment, (2) recreational companionship, (3) an attractive spouse, (4) domestic support, and (5) admiration.[4]

The more deposits a wife makes into her husband's love bank by meeting these needs, the more addicted he will be to her. But if she fails to make those deposits, he will not only lose interest in her, he will begin to resent her.

For example, several years ago I briefly counseled a couple in which the wife was outwardly very attractive but rather cold toward her husband. Because of unresolved issues in her childhood, she viewed sex as bad and only necessary for procreation. Once they had their children, she stopped having any interest in meeting her husband's sexual needs.

He began to withdraw from her. This only accelerated her coldness toward him, which made every other struggle in their marriage larger. Eventually, it came out that he was having an affair with a woman from his office. Their friends and family were surprised that the woman who stole his heart was not nearly as pretty as his wife. But they failed to realize that she was much more eager than his wife was to meet his sexual needs.

I've found that if I ask a husband to tell me what activities make deposits into his wife's love bank, he generally responds with a blank expression. When asked to list his wife's basic needs, again he is stumped by the question. He has simply never considered it.

James Dobson found that women with unmet needs suffer from what he calls "the Ds" of despair, discouragement, disinterest, distress, despondency, and depression.[5] He found that low self-esteem was the most troubling problem expressed by the women he surveyed. This lack of esteem has been multiplied and increased as society has increasingly devalued the role of a stay-at-home wife and mother, and has elevated physical beauty over character or intelligence.

The wives surveyed by Dobson also stated that they were depressed because of fatigue, especially after the children came along. Between working a job, raising children, buying groceries, and keeping the home clean and running effectively, they have several full-time jobs. This was exhausting and ultimately depressing.

Dobson's survey revealed that another primary problem area for wives was "loneliness, isolation, and boredom." Yet another depression-inducing frustration was "the lack of romantic love in their marriage." In summary, wives were saying: "I'm depressed because I don't like myself; I'm exhausted by trying to keep up; I have no meaningful relationships; and I'm not close to my husband."

Harley observed that a wife's primary needs were fivefold as well: (1) affection, (2) conversation, (3) trust induced through openness and honesty, (4) stable financial support, and (5) family commitment through being a good father.[6] In other words, a wife needs clear expressions of love from her husband.

Wives Need Love

Just as men deeply need respect, women deeply need love. In the remainder of this chapter, we will discuss how husbands can best love their wives. Simply stated, husbands are commanded to give love-saturated servant leadership to their wives. The obvious picture for how husbands love their wives is Christ's love for the church:

> *For the husband is the head of the wife as Christ is the head of the church, his body, of which he is the Savior. Now as the church submits to Christ, so also wives should submit to their husbands in everything. Husbands, love your wives, just as Christ loved the church and gave himself up for her to make her holy, cleansing her by the washing with water through the word, and to present her to himself as a radiant church, without stain or wrinkle or any other blemish, but holy and blameless.*
> *In this same way, husbands ought to love their wives as their own bodies. He who loves his wife loves himself. After all, no one ever hated their own body, but they feed and care for their body, just as Christ does the church. . . . However, each one of you also must love his wife as he loves himself.*
> EPHESIANS 5:23–29, 33 NIV

From this passage, we can identify four key elements of a husband's love for his wife: leadership, sacrifice, godliness, and unconditional devotion.

Leadership: "The husband is the head of the wife as Christ is the head of the church." Too many wives are frustrated by husbands who fail to lead in the home. Leadership is not a position but a responsibility. Leaders take initiative. They do their duty. They meet their obligations. They display the courage of their convictions. Leaders have a plan. They follow a clear direction. They provide guidance. When a husband does these things, a wife feels loved and cared for.

Sacrifice: "Christ loved the church and gave himself up for her." Husbands who sacrifice for their wives communicate love to their wives. Wives who don't feel loved by their husbands secretly (and sometimes not so secretly) resent their husbands for being self-centered.

Godliness: "To make her holy, cleansing her by the washing with water through the word, and to present her to himself as a radiant church, without stain or wrinkle or any other blemish, but holy and blameless." God the Father has called husbands to cooperate with Him in helping wives reach their spiritual potential. How many good-hearted women would love to have a husband who will step up and become the spiritual leader in the home! Husbands should pray *for* and *with* their wives. They should lead them to church. They should take responsibility for having family prayer times.

Unconditional Devotion: "Husbands, love your wives. . . . Each one of you also must love his wife as he loves himself." Marriages starve from lack of love. Your wife needs your consistent, unconditional love as much as she needs food, water, and oxygen.

There are several significant expressions of the love a wife needs from her husband.

The following expressions, if consistently given to a wife, will create a much happier and more fulfilling marriage.

1. Adoration

Your wife needs to know that she is highly valued and is number one on your priority list, second only to God in your life.

2. Affection

As a body needs food, a woman's emotions need touch. Your wife needs to feel close and connected to you. Affection from her husband symbolizes security, protection, comfort, and approval for a wife. You need to tenderly listen to her, talk to her, touch her, hug her, and hold her *apart from* times of sexual intimacy.

3. Authenticity

She needs you to open up to her and give her consistent and unobstructed communication. Share your life, thoughts, feelings, hopes, fears, and dreams with her.

4. Approval

One of the most devastating emotions a wife can feel is lack of approval from her mate. She needs to know that you like her *as she is*. She needs to feel that you will take her side and support her in her role. Your wife needs to feel understood. Do not try to fix her when she is upset. Don't give answers or solutions right away. Just comfort her and listen.

5. Assurance

Your wife needs reassurance that you love her, that you are loyal to her, and that you are committed to her "no matter what." She needs to know that you will protect and provide for her and the family.

6. Attention

Your wife spells love a-t-t-e-n-t-i-o-n. The opposite of love isn't so much hate as it is apathy. Often the worst form of rejection is to be ignored. Most men know very little about their wives because they don't pay attention. Someone has observed that if a husband does not pay attention, he will pay alimony. Your wife needs you to pay attention to her. You need to wake up and notice some of the vast array of things she does to love and serve you and the children. She needs you to listen when she talks.

7. Appreciation

Your wife needs to feel appreciated by you. Practice saying words of thanks, praise, and appreciation at least once a day. Make her birthday and your wedding anniversary very special occasions.

Give Him a Target to Hit

Not all of the needs listed above are true of every wife. And most guys can't remember all seven needs anyway, let alone feel capable of meeting them all the time. Therefore, it is imperative that a wife give her husband a target to hit—her target.

I suggest that both husbands and wives read through the above mentioned needs and then discuss them. Aim to have a list of three or four needs that are especially important for your mate at this time.

Then, as you seek to meet each other's needs, be sure to respond positively to your mate's efforts.

Be patient. It may take a while for your spouse to focus adequately on your needs. In the meantime, make sure you're focusing adequately on your spouse's needs. It may also take some "close but not quite it" attempts before you both become skilled at meeting each other's needs in the way you want them met.

Notes

1. Willard F. Harley, *His Needs, Her Needs* (Grand Rapids, MI: Fleming Revel, 1986), 19.

2. Ibid., 18.

3. Emerson Eggerichs, *Love and Respect* (Brentwood, TN: Integrity Publishing, 2004), 6.

4. Harley, *His Needs, Her Needs*, 12.

5. James Dobson, *What Wives Wish Their Husbands Knew about Women* (Wheaton, IL: Tyndale House Publishers, 1975), 15.

6. Harley, *His Needs, Her Needs*, 13.

Chapter 7

Ignite the Romance

D o you deeply long to love lavishly, be loved passionately, and to see this love grow through the years?

Of course you do.

And God desires this for you as well.

After all, He is the one who invented the mysterious attraction we have to the opposite sex, along with romance, marriage, intimacy, and the sex drive. God is undeniably the foremost expert on these issues.

Beyond that, God has already recorded a great deal of practical and explicit information about romance, intimacy, love, and sex. That's right, I said *sex*. In fact, God has devoted an entire book of the Bible to these issues. He has given us an instruction manual dedicated to the cultivation of romance, intimacy, love, and sex. It is found in the wisdom section of the Old Testament and is called the Song of Solomon.

The Song of Solomon is a love poem or song written by the world's wisest man. It consists of fifteen reflections of a married woman, King Solomon's queen. These poems are flashbacks of the events leading to marriage, the wedding night, and their first years together. In them we learn the value of, and the means to, intensifying intimacy in marriage.

Secret #7
Ignite the romance.

What Is Romance?

When the Romans ruled the world, Latin was the official language of the empire. All formal documents were written in Latin.

But when common people spoke, they did not use Latin. They used their native languages. When they sat around the fire and told stories of love and bravery, they did not use Latin. When they talked with their family around the dinner table or with their mate later that night in bed, they used the languages of the heart.

These heart languages eventually came to be known as the Romance languages. The term *romantic* came to be used for informal speech and earthy expressions of passion, as opposed to formal, legal language.

Today, when we marry, we make a formal agreement with our mate. Yet marriage was meant to be much, much more than merely a formal arrangement. It is intended to be a passionate, vibrant, intimate adventure. Solomon knew this, which is why he speaks in poetic romantic terms to his bride in the love poem we call the Song of Solomon.

How to Ignite the Romance in Your Marriage

It is beyond the scope of this book to provide a complete commentary on Solomon's fascinating love poem, but I will focus on the highlights that allowed the couple in the poem to experience exciting marital love, intimacy, and passionate sex. We'll see several significant commitments that built their intimacy and ignited their sexual ardor. Let me warn you that some of these scripture passages are very graphic. (Hebrew boys were not allowed to read the Song of Solomon until they were at least twelve years old.)

I believe that as you practice these commitments, they will absolutely help ignite the romance in your marriage. Within the covenant of marriage, sexual intimacy is a beautiful gift that God desires us to enjoy fully (Hebrews 13:4).

1. *Express love fully and frequently.*

There is an old story of a married couple coming to their pastor for counseling. He asked them to describe the problems they saw with their marriage. The wife immediately piped up regarding her husband, "He does not love me."

"Why would you say that?" asked the pastor.

"He never tells me that he loves me," the wife replied.

"Well, do you love your wife?" the pastor asked the husband.

"I do love her," the husband replied.

"Then why don't you tell her?" the pastor asked.

"I told her I love her the day I married her," he said slowly. "If I change my mind, I'll let her know."

The husband's failure to express his love was killing his marriage. This is the exact opposite of the couple described in the Song of Solomon. From the very beginning, they expressed their love to each other verbally, positively, and emotionally. Listen to the passionate romance expressed as they speak to one another.

First we see the husband exclaiming, "Oh, my dear friend! You're so beautiful!" (Song of Solomon 1:15 MSG). To which the wife replies, "And you, my dear lover—you're so handsome! And the bed we share is like a forest glen" (1:16 MSG). They give rich, romantic words to their emotions.

Later in the book, we eavesdrop on their wedding night. The new husband slowly undresses his new bride while expressing robust appreciation for everything he sees. He positively comments on every aspect of her body. As you read his words, ask yourself what woman would not like to be so lavishly described and enjoyed by her husband.

You're so beautiful, my darling, so beautiful, and your dove eyes are veiled by your hair as it flows and shimmers. . . . Your smile is generous and full—expressive and strong and clean. Your lips are jewel red, your mouth elegant and inviting, your veiled cheeks soft and radiant. The smooth, lithe lines of your neck command notice—all heads turn in awe and admiration! Your breasts are like fawns [young and taut]. . . The sweet, fragrant curves of your body, the soft, spiced contours of your flesh invite me, and I come. I stay until dawn breathes its light and night slips away. You're beautiful from head to toe, my dear love, beautiful beyond compare, absolutely flawless.

SONG OF SOLOMON 4:1–7 MSG

Their exuberant expressiveness does not end there. They're just getting started. They move from describing how attractive they find each other to how they make each other feel. Notice how they pile on the imagery to convey the picture of sheer delight in their mate's love.

You've captured my heart, dear friend. You looked at me, and I fell in love. One look my way and I was hopelessly in love! How beautiful your love, dear, dear friend—far more pleasing than a fine, rare wine, your fragrance more exotic than select spices. The kisses of your lips are honey, my love, every syllable you speak a delicacy to savor.

SONG OF SOLOMON 4:9–11 MSG

Wise couples are committed to saying often *that* they love each other. They also creatively express *why* they love each other.

2. *Enjoy intimacy thoroughly.*

When it comes to making love, Gary Smalley says, "Men are microwaves and women are Crock-Pots." Men can be ready for sex in moments. Women heat up more slowly, requiring time and tenderness. Men physically enjoy the act of sex and the physical release. They feel close *after* the act. Women have a hard time appreciating intercourse without a sense of kindness, gentleness, and closeness *before* the act.

As you read through the words expressed in Song of Solomon chapter four, please realize that there is more going on here than just talking. The husband is obviously engaged in slow, romantic foreplay. He describes gently touching his bride's eyelids and then her lips. He deeply kisses her mouth. He slowly nuzzles her cheeks and kisses her neck. Next, he tenderly touches her breasts. Slowly he moves to the gentle curves of her stomach, her hips, and inner thighs.

He is in no hurry to get to the main event. In fact, he appears to be deeply enjoying the whole process—and, make no mistake, so is she. With both his words and his touch, she is enraptured. As a result, she makes herself completely available to him.

In the Bible, a man's sexuality is described as a fountain and a woman's as a garden. The husband now describes his new bride as a "secret garden," which means that she is a virgin. Notice the joyful delight he expresses in her purity and virginity.

Dear lover and friend, you're a secret garden,
a private and pure fountain. Body and soul,
you are paradise, a whole orchard of succulent fruits.
SONG OF SOLOMON 4:12 MGS

Her response is important. Because he has been slow and tender, nurturing and cherishing her with his passionate expressions of love, she is very responsive to him.

Oh, let my lover enter his garden!
Yes, let him eat the fine, ripe fruits.
SONG OF SOLOMON 4:16 MSG

The young bride says to her husband the words he has been waiting to hear: "Come and have all the sex you want. Come to my garden and eat your fill of my fruit."[1]

Later in the Song of Solomon, we have another description of the couple's lovemaking that is every bit as provocative as the earlier passages. Because the husband has made his wife feel deeply appreciated and sought after, she makes herself fully available to him to enjoy. She plans a romantic getaway for just the two of them, where she can focus on giving herself completely to him.

I am my lover's. I'm all he wants. I'm all the world to him!
Come, dear lover—let's tramp through the countryside. Let's sleep at some
wayside inn. . . . And there I'll give myself to you, my love to your love!
SONG OF SOLOMON 7:9–13 MSG

In marriage, couples must surrender their bodies to each other for *the other's* pleasure (1 Corinthians 7:1–4). In the Song of Solomon, notice the bride's positive attitude regarding sexual intimacy.

> *My lover is already on his way to his garden, to browse among the flowers, touching the colors and forms. I am my lover's and my lover is mine. He caresses the sweet-smelling flowers.*
> SONG OF SOLOMON 6:2–3 MSG

Wise couples are committed to each other's pleasure above their own, especially in the bedroom. The husband focuses on his wife and gives her great tenderness. The wife gives her husband eager responsiveness and availability.

3. *Experience love extravagantly.*

One neglected aspect of too many marriages, and especially Christian marriages, is the notion of extravagance. I think the Puritan notion of thriftiness and simplicity has been mistakenly adopted as a reason to skimp on our marriages.

This obviously is not the case in the Song of Solomon. As we have seen, this love poem is a chock-full of eloquent expressions, extreme exaggeration, hyperbole, rich imagery, and excessive words.

But the extravagance extends beyond words. In the first chapter of the song, the husband mentions giving his bride expensive gifts of jewelry.

Pendant earrings line the elegance of your cheeks; strands of jewels
illumine the curve of your throat. I'm making jewelry for you,
gold and silver jewelry that will mark and accent your beauty.

SONG OF SOLOMON 1:9–11 MSG

When Cathy and I were engaged, the best I could afford to give her was my grandmother's wedding ring. It was distinct and suited her long fingers nicely. She was gracious to accept and wear it gladly. But it was old and brittle and the prongs often broke.

By the time of our twenty-fifth anniversary, we were in a financial position to upgrade to a very pretty diamond. I can't tell you how happy I was to be able to give it to her. For us, it was extravagant. But Cathy loves it, and I love the fact that I could give it to her, because she certainly is worth all that and so much more.

Throughout the Song of Solomon, we read of fragrant spices and perfumes. Though some of these descriptions are best understood as euphemisms for erotic pleasures, some are also speaking of literal fragrances. Many of the perfumes described are rare, exotic, and extremely expensive. The point being that nothing was spared to make the most of the romantic aspects of their relationship.

Wise couples keep dating after they say, "I do." They know that if anything is worth the expense, it is their marriage. They know that saving up for a nice meal out or a fun weekend in a charming bed-and-breakfast is worth the investment.

4. *Exalt all the elements of marital love.*

While the Song of Solomon is a love poem that celebrates the joys of sexual intimacy within marriage, there is more to it than that. We see the couple facing and resolving conflicts and practicing other relationship-building habits that enhance the entire relationship—and not merely in the bedroom.

It has been said that "good sex is icing on the cake of a good marriage." How true.

One of the clues to the multi-sided strength of the overall marriage seen in the Song of Solomon is the names the lovers gave each other and what they signify.

My lover, my friend (5:16): I like the fact that the two terms *lover* and *friend* are linked together. In marriage, they complement and build up each other. As the friendship deepens, the intimacy grows. As the intimacy grows, the friendship deepens. Your mate needs to become your best friend.

My sister, my bride (4:8–10, 12): The words *sister* and *bride* speak of kindred spirits or close companions. Never underestimate the power of deepening companionship when it comes to enhancing intimacy.

People get married because they like to spend time together. This mustn't stop after you get married.

My male work and business colleagues cannot understand why I never learned to golf. As a church planter, father, and young husband, I never had the time or money, although Cathy would have let me. But now I honestly would rather spend my days
off hiking or biking with Cathy than chasing a little white ball around with the guys.

My darling/my love (1:9; 2:2, 10; 4:1, 7); *my beloved/my lover* (1:14–16; 2:3, 8–10,16–17; 4:16; 5:4–6, 8, 10; 6:2; 7:9–11; 8:14); *the one my heart loves* (3:1–4): The Song of Solomon is saturated with affectionate words, attitudes, and actions.

Guys especially need to be reminded that "sex starts in the kitchen." We should give our wives loving words often throughout the day. We should give them hugs, touches, squeezes, pats, and kisses at times other than when we're in the bedroom. We must continue to "date" our wives and look for opportunities as often as possible to snuggle and cuddle with them.

My dove (2:14; 5:2; 6:9): A dove is a very beautiful, gentle, and sensitive bird. The pet name "my dove" reveals how sensitive these two lovers were toward each other.

My beautiful one (2:10*), my flawless one* (5:2), *my perfect one,* (2:14; 6:9): These lovers in the Song of Solomon carefully use their words to communicate acceptance and approval of each other. After we are married, our mate's opinion of us is of prime importance. In other words, as long as my wife communicates to me that she thinks I am attractive, I feel good about myself. If I ever feel like she does not accept me or approve of me, I'm crushed.

I am my beloveds, and his desire is toward me (7:10): The bride in the Song of Solomon was very confident and secure in her husband's love. Emotionally, physically, financially, and sexually, she was certain that she was safe and that his only interest was her.

Wise couples understand that enjoyable sexual intimacy is the overflow of a healthy relationship. They learn to give their mate friendship, companionship, and affection outside the bedroom. They are committed to making their mate feel approved, accepted, and secure.

5. *Exclude sex outside of marriage.*

Sexual intimacy is a very good, highly honored, mightily mysterious, and intensely intoxicating gift that God gave us as a powerful marriage enhancer. But He is very clear that this gift is to be enjoyed only in the loving bond of covenantal marriage (Hebrews 13:4).

Song of Solomon describes the importance of purity within marriage from two angles. First, the bride in the poem gives at least three clear warnings to her unmarried sisters. This warning is repeated in contexts that make it clear she is warning them not to allow premarital sex to rob them of the greater joys of marital sex (2:7), cloud their ability to choose the right mate (3:5), or hinder their ability to resolve marital conflicts (8:4).

Second, on several occasions, the love poem is adamant that the full joy of sexual intimacy is reserved for "the secret garden banquet," which is closed to all but your mate (4:12–16).

Wise couples focus all their sexual energies on each other. This includes not only what they do with their bodies but also their minds and emotions. Sex is never considered outside the marriage covenant.

Two Key Words for Greater Sexual Intimacy

Great sex is a matter of *romance* and *responsiveness*. Husbands, remember that your wife needs *romance*. Take the lead. If necessary, *plan* your spontaneity—that is, think ahead about what you can do to make your wife feel loved. Then *act*. Be extravagant. Bring her flowers and candy for no reason other than that you love her. Continue to date.

Wives, remember that your husband needs *responsiveness*. I'm told that in Victorian England, brides-to-be were coached to "lie on their back and think of the queen," in order to "endure the wedding night." No wonder their husbands had mistresses! Wise wives actively respond to their husband's romantic attempts and sexual advances. You should be the one to flirt with and pursue him.

When husbands focus on being more romantic, and wives focus on being more responsive, romance is ignited, passion is renewed, and love is deepened.

Notes

1. Tommy Nelson, *The Book of Romance: What Solomon Says about Love, Sex, and Intimacy* (Nashville, TN: Thomas Nelson, 1998), 102.

Chapter 8

Affair-Proof Your Marriage

A few years ago, I received an e-mail from a friend saying he was resigning his position as lead pastor of his church. This was a church he had started and that was off to an extremely successful first several years. They had captured the attention of their community, built a super facility, and had hundreds of people participating in their weekly gatherings.

The e-mail went on to state that he needed to resign in order to spend more time with his family and work on his marriage. It turned out that adultery was the issue. He had been cheating on his wife.

The discovery of his lack of integrity was devastating for his children, his wife, his health, his church, and the Lord's reputation in the community. Those closest to him wrestled with intense feelings of shock, anger, betrayal, and deep hurt. He had sinned, cheated, denied, lied, and deceived.

I kept thinking, *this did not have to happen. Of all people, he knew better. Many people would have gladly helped. It never had to come to this.*

But it had. His church and family were left to struggle through the aftermath of this awful, ugly episode.

"Until Adultery Do Us Part"

God has an ideal for sex: it is to be fully enjoyed within the bounds of a strong, committed, well-rounded marriage. Whenever sex occurs outside of marriage, not only is the ideal missed but problems arise. Guilt, mistrust, and pain are just a few of the consequences.

No one gets married with the expectation of being cheated on by their mate. You marry with the dream of both spouses being loyal and faithful until "death do us part." Unfortunately, that is not always the case.

Studies have found that as many as two out of three married people have an extramarital affair. We know that as many as 90 percent of divorces in longstanding marriages involve infidelity at some time during the marriage.

As we've said, God designed marriage to be a lifelong covenant of fidelity and purity. He takes marital loyalty seriously and strongly prohibits adultery—in fact, He includes it as one of the Ten Commandments that He wrote on the stone tablets that Moses carried down from Mt. Sinai (Deuteronomy 5:1, 18, 22).

Adultery is never the right thing to do. It is always a sin. It is a sin against society, against marriage, against your children, and against your mate.

But that's not all.

Adultery is a sin against yourself. Solomon warned that adultery ultimately destroys the adulterer (Proverbs 6:32). Paul warned that it is a sin against your own body (1 Corinthians 6).

But there is yet more.

Most important, adultery is a sin against God. Joseph refused to enjoy sex with another man's wife, because it was "great wickedness and *a sin against God*" (Genesis 39:9, emphasis added).

Remember, God's commands are not restrictions on our happiness; they are expressions of His love. God says no to sex outside of marriage because He loves us, He loves our mates, and He loves our kids.

God loves families and marriages so much that He made adultery punishable by death when He gave Israel the Law (Deuteronomy 22:22; Leviticus 20:10). Under the New Covenant of grace, God still warns that adulterers and fornicators will be severely judged (Hebrews 13:4).

Immorality is always very costly and spiritually deadly. No one can afford to pay its crushing price. One hour of pleasure can lead to years of agony. Wise Christian spouses take the necessary steps to safeguard their marriages.

Secret #8
Affair-proof your marriage.

Commitments for Affair-Proofing Your Marriage

After reading my friend's painful account of resigning from his church because of moral failure, I decided to write down the nonnegotiable commitments I had made to Cathy in order to fulfill the promise I made to be faithful to her until death do us part. Adherence to these three commitments will prevent adultery and build marital intimacy.

1. *I will erect barriers to adultery.*
When Proverbs warns of the dangers of giving in to the seductions of the adulteress, it concludes with the command to stay as far away from adultery as possible!

My son, pay attention to my wisdom; listen carefully to my wise counsel. . . . For the lips of an immoral woman are as sweet as honey, and her mouth is smoother than oil. But in the end she is as bitter as poison, as dangerous as a double-edged sword. Her feet go down to death; her steps lead straight to the grave. For she cares nothing about the path to life. . . . So now, my sons, listen to me. Never stray from what I am about to say: **Stay away from her! Don't go near the door of her house!**

PROVERBS 5:1–8 NLT (EMPHASIS ADDED)

In order to follow this advice, I choose to erect some commonsense fences to protect myself, my reputation, my wife, my children, my ministry, my church, and the name of Jesus. I have witnessed too many cases of devastation caused by someone who got too close to adultery and ended up in an affair, so I want my fences to be high and thick and hard to get around.

Bear in mind, these are the planks of *my* blockade against adultery. If you find my barriers too restrictive, I suggest that you and your mate come up with your own set of barriers and follow them.

Five Barriers to Adultery

a. Never be alone with a person of the opposite sex.

It is simple really—*if* I am never physically alone with a woman who is not my wife, *then* I cannot possibly commit adultery. I extend this rule to include not being isolated with a woman for any length of time for any reason behind closed doors. And my office door has a window in it. I also don't counsel women alone. I have either Cathy or a female staff member join me. I won't eat lunch one-on-one in a restaurant with a woman other than my wife. I also won't ride in a car alone with a woman other than my wife.

b. Always wear your ring.

Have you noticed that people on the prowl don't wear their wedding ring? Wearing your ring makes it clear that you are not available and not interested—and it will help protect you from temptation you don't need.

c. Always build up your mate and marriage in public.

When in a conversation with someone of the opposite sex, intentionally try to inject something positive about your mate into the conversation as soon and often as possible. That makes it clear that you are happily married. I make a point of doing this because I want it to be known that I am very content.

Never complain about your marriage or your mate to a person of the opposite sex. Don't ever joke about your mate or your marriage with someone of the opposite sex.

Keep a good picture of your mate and one of your children on your desk. Include your mate in your Facebook profile picture. Put a photo of your mate and you, or just your mate, on your laptop screen saver and cell phone.

Don't be afraid to show your spouse appropriate affection in public.

d. Never share personal, emotional feelings with any person of the opposite sex (other than your spouse).

Adulterers almost always commit *emotional* adultery before they commit physical adultery. The Internet has made it easier for married people to share their intimate feelings with others through the various avenues of social media.

A man in my church carried on an emotional affair over the Internet with a woman who was a business contact of his in another city. This went on for more than a year, until one weekend when he told his wife he was going to visit his mother but instead flew across the country to spend the weekend with his "soul mate." It all began with a "harmless e-mail," in which he shared a bit too much information with someone other than his wife.

As we counseled him and his wife through the aftermath of his sin, I made the commitment to always be certain that Cathy had full access to my e-mail. I have received a few questionable e-mails since then, and I have been careful to make sure that Cathy has seen them.

e. Be careful how you dress and how you touch or talk to persons of the opposite sex.

Generally, men respond to looks and women respond to words and to touch. Practically, this means that a woman needs to be careful how she dresses, and a man needs to be careful what he says and does. Regardless of whether a woman wears a wedding band, if her skirt is too short, her top too tight, or her neckline too low, she is sending the message that she is willing and available. Men will see a green light, regardless of her intentions.

A man needs to be very careful how he speaks to or touches a woman. She will read the tone of his voice and respond to his words. And she'll notice where he looks.

Don't ever flirt with another woman. Be careful about mentioning her new hairstyle or new dress, or that she has lost weight or looks nice.

A man needs to be especially careful about touching a woman other than his wife. Grabbing her hand, giving a hug, or patting her on the shoulder can be innocent or it can be seductive. Be careful—and when in doubt, don't.

2. *I will choose not to lust.*

We live in a society that is crazed by sex. Men, especially, fantasize about sex, though women do, too. One recent survey of eight hundred active church members and leaders found that 15 percent of the men and 11 percent of the women admitted to marital infidelity, and 49 percent had viewed pornography in the past year. I can only imagine how many more had lusted after someone other than their mate.

I seriously doubt if anyone ever committed adultery without first having the thought. We must stop the process before it starts.

The Bible is very clear about the dangers of lust. For example, Proverbs warns that what starts with lust leads to adultery, which results in serious pain.

> Don't lust for her beauty. Don't let her coy glances seduce you.
> For a prostitute will bring you to poverty, but sleeping with another
> man's wife will cost you your life. Can a man scoop a flame into his
> lap and not have his clothes catch on fire? Can he walk on hot coals
> and not blister his feet? So it is with the man who sleeps with
> another man's wife. He who embraces her will not go unpunished.
> PROVERBS 6:25–29 NLT

In the New Testament, Jesus equates lust with mental adultery. He warns that lust will lead to corruption.

You know the next commandment pretty well, too: "Don't go to bed with another's spouse." But don't think you've preserved your virtue simply by staying out of bed. Your heart can be corrupted by lust even quicker than your body. Those leering looks you think nobody notices—they also corrupt.

MATTHEW 5:27–28 MSG

Job, in speaking of maintaining his integrity, stated that he made a commitment to stop adultery before it started: "I made a covenant with my eyes not to look lustfully at a young woman" (Job 31:1 NIV).

We can prevent adultery by blocking lust. In order to stay pure, as a man and as a husband, I have made the following commitments.

I Will Never. . .

- look at a pornographic website.
- read a trashy or questionable novel.
- visit an "adult" bookstore.
- go to a so-called gentleman's club.
- look at a pornographic magazine.
- watch an "adult" video or movie.
- look closely at a woman (other than my wife) below her chin.
- engage in a personal phone call or e-mail exchange with a woman other than my wife without my wife's knowledge.
- be alone with a woman other than my wife in any setting, at any time, for any reason.
- share my personal or emotional feelings with any woman other than my wife.
- view women as anything other than people for whom Jesus bled and died.

3. *I will invest in my marriage.*

The easiest way to avoid adultery is to be so over-the-top in love with your mate that no one else could possibly pry you away. Proverbs advises:

> *Enjoy the wife you married as a young man! Lovely as an angel, beautiful as a rose— don't ever quit taking delight in her body. Never take her love for granted! Why would you trade enduring intimacies for cheap thrills with a whore? for dalliance with a promiscuous stranger?*
>
> PROVERBS 5:18–20 MSG

Wise couples take all the energy, creativity, effort, initiative, time, and money that other people spend having an affair and pour it into romancing each other.

"If You Must Have an Affair, Have It with Your Mate"

Several years ago, I counseled a Christian businessman who was succumbing to the sweet seductions of a young woman who worked in his office. He was on the verge of ruining his marriage, his family, and his testimony. He told me how she had become all he could think about, and how her perfume lingered in his memory. He spoke of the sound of her voice and her laugh. He told of how much fun it was flirting with her, writing her notes, and ingeniously finding opportunities when they could be together.

I listened for a while until I couldn't take it anymore. I bluntly pointed out that he was being blind and selfish. Then I called him to repent of the sin he was on the edge of committing, because it was hurting God and would crush his wife and kids. He needed to realize that he was about to make this young lady from work into a fornicator. I pointed out that, even if his wife "did not know what was going on," she had to know that his heart was not fully hers. This was probably why she seemed "so distant and depressed lately," as he had told me earlier.

To his credit, he responded. He wept like a baby.

Then he looked at me and asked, "What do I do now?"

"First," I said, "you must break off all contact with this other woman."

"But it will hurt her feelings," he said.

"At this point," I said, "her feelings are not nearly as important as your integrity, your family, your marriage, and your *wife's* feelings." Then we discussed how best to go about severing all ties with the young woman.

He understood and agreed. "What else should I do?" he asked.

"If in your self-centered midlife crisis you must have an affair, have it with your wife," I said. "God has *already* given you a lovely woman with nice perfume, a lovely voice, and a sweet laugh. If you took all of the creativity, money, time, effort, and energy you've been spending on flirting with and pursuing this young woman, and spent it wooing your wife instead, I bet she would no longer be so distant and depressed."

"I see," he said slowly, considering the idea.

"When was the last time you bought your wife flowers or jewelry or wrote her a love note or skipped out from work early to meet her in the park?"

"Oh, well I see," he said. "That would make sense, *if* I felt like it. But wouldn't doing those things be hypocritical if I don't feel them?"

"It would be much less hypocritical than calling yourself an honorable man while you are plotting to cheat on your wife and fornicate with this young woman," I said.

"Keeping your covenant with your mate is right and honors God, *whether you feel like it or not*," I continued. "Remember, in the Bible, you are commanded to love your wife, whether you feel like it or not. Nine times out of ten, *after* you do the right thing, you will start feeling it."

"So I should fake it till I feel it," he said.

"The point is not to fake it," I said. "Listen, I believe that if you spend the next month ardently flirting with, dating, wooing, and pursuing your wife, you will find that the romantic feelings you had when you first got married will return."

The Rest of the Story

To his credit, he seriously heeded my words. I met with him weekly to coach him through severing his relationship with the woman from work and wooing his wife's heart. He went all out doing everything I suggested, and God graciously worked in his marriage. Little by little, his wife began to respond and his heart began to change.

By the end of the month, I saw him and his wife entering the church lobby laughing and smiling. She glowed as she clutched his arm and he hugged her close. She giggled and told me that he had taken her away for a night at an elegant hotel, and they had not had so much fun together since they first got married. She proudly showed me a new bracelet he had bought her.

"I don't know what has gotten into him," she said. "But I hope it never goes away!"

Chapter 9

Fill Your Mate's Tank

Cathy and I bought our first home in the middle of winter. When spring came, I found that the lawn I had inherited was about 60 percent grass, 30 percent dandelions, and 10 percent other weeds. Because I was focused at the time on starting a church, I soon fell behind on my lawn mowing and the weeds began to take over.

It seemed that whenever I did have time to mow the grass, it was raining so I couldn't do it. Before long, our lawn began to look like a jungle.

Finally one evening, I had a little window of time before it got dark. It was supposed to rain again that night, so this was my only chance. I opened the shed to get out the lawn mower that had come with the house. I rolled it out onto the driveway, raised the deck of the blade because the grass was so high, pushed the choke, and pulled the cord. *Vrroooommm,* it started up right away.

As I quickly began to cut my way around the edges, the mower started to sputter. I gave it more air and kept on cutting. It sputtered again and gasped. *Puh, Puh, Puh Puhhhh. . .*and it died.

I rolled it over to the driveway again, pushed the choke, and pulled the cord. Nothing.

I tried again and again. Still nothing.

I figured I had flooded it, so I waited. As I stood there, the sky got darker and darker. I could feel night falling and a storm blowing in.

I pulled the cord again and again, nothing.

Again. . .nothing.

Again. . .nothing.

I said a prayer.

I pulled the cord again, and again nothing.

I said some bad things to the lawn mower. That didn't help either.

About this time, Cathy peeked out the door. "I thought you were going to mow the lawn," she said. "It's getting dark and they said it will rain."

I told her the lawn mower had died on me. "Well," she said, "the people we bought the house from said it was only a year old. You must be doing something wrong."

"Look," I said, more than a little irritated. "It *was* running and it quit."

"Oh," she said. "Maybe it's out of gas."

"Out of gas!" I said. "It can't be out of gas." *What does she know?* I thought.

"Did you look?" she asked.

"No, I did not look," I said.

"Do you want me to show you where the gas tank is?" she asked.

"No, I can do it," I replied. I grabbed the first cap I saw, read the word GAS on it, and twisted it with authority.

I peeked inside. It was dry as a bone.

"Is it out of gas?" Cathy asked.

"Yes," I said weakly.

"Better get more in it. It's getting dark," she warned.

"I know!" I replied. Then I stomped back to the shed and grabbed the gas can. *Wow.* I thought. *This is amazingly light. This new metal is practically weightless.*

I opened the lid and a moth flew out. That should have been a clue. I tipped the can up and nothing came out. Not a drop.

"Is it empty?" Cathy asked.

"Yes," I fumed.

"What are you going to do?" she asked. "It's getting dark."

"I know."

"Why don't you ask Tony?" she said.

Tony was our next door neighbor. He was a nice guy who had grown up in Vietnam. I had talked to him on several occasions. The only trouble was that I could not understand much of what he said.

I rang his doorbell and he came to the door. I asked him if I could please borrow some gas for my lawn mower.

He shook his head like he did not understand. This went on for a while as the sky kept getting darker and darker.

Finally he understood enough to take me out to his garage. I pointed at the gas can. He smiled. I picked it up and shook it gently.

It was empty. He got a big smile on his face as we broke the communication barrier. But neither of us had gasoline.

Obviously, I did not get the lawn mowed that night; but the next day I got gas and checked the oil. It also was empty. When I sharpened the blade, changed the air filter, and filled both tanks, the mower ran just great.

Even though I did not get that lawn mowed that night, I learned some valuable lessons—lessons that apply not only to lawn mowers and weeds but also to marriage. The big lesson was this: just as a lawnmower with an empty tank won't run, neither will a marriage.

Secret #9
Fill your spouse's love tank.

1. We have a love tank with every person in our lives, especially with our mates.

It took me years to figure this out. Every relationship is affected by a "tank of expectations," especially marriage.

Too many couples run into severe relationship problems before they ever recognize this simple truth. They end up fighting or sitting in a counselor's office saying of their mate, "I have no feelings for him (or her) anymore. There is nothing left." What they are really saying is that their relational tank has run dry.

2. The more important the relationship, the larger the love tank we need to fill.

A relationship with a casual acquaintance has a very small love tank. Relationships with siblings are larger, especially when you and they are living at home. This is also true of your relationship with your parents. Your relationship with your kids has a large love tank to fill, especially when the kids are still at home or living in the area. But no love tank is larger or more significant than the one you have with your mate.

3. When the relational tank is full, the relationship runs better.

A full-tank relationship will hum along. It does not sputter when the grass gets high or the weeds get thick. It cuts right through problems.

But when the love tank runs low, the slightest problem can cause the engine to sputter and the blade to bind up. If the tank is not attended to, it will run dry and the relationship will suffer.

4. The relational tank is filled or drained by the other person's reception of our actions, attitudes, and words.

Every interaction has the potential to either add to or subtract from our love tanks. As my wife and I interact, if she sees our interaction as positive, I have added to her tank. If she sees it as negative, regardless of my intent, I have subtracted from her tank. If I thought it was a positive interaction, but she thought it was negative, it was negative. My tank might have been filled, but hers was drained.

This is a powerful truth. The way I say good-bye to Cathy when I leave for work can either add to or subtract from our relationship. The way I act when I come home in the evening either adds to or subtracts from our relationship. All my actions and interactions affect the level of the love tank in that relationship.

5. Because we cannot control draining events, we must intentionally initiate filling events.

In any marriage, there will be certain draining events that are out of our control. We cannot necessarily control when we'll get sick or when we'll have to work late or whether we'll be downsized out of a job. These things happen, and they limit our ability to build our relationships.

Therefore, because I know to expect some negative events beyond my control, I must intentionally initiate as many love tank–filling elements as possible in my marriage. But what are they?

Marriage Relationship Tank Fillers

The writers of the New Testament understood a great deal about relationships. They spoke not only of our relationships with God but also with one another. In fact, there are more than three dozen "words of advice" about relationship building with others. We call them the "one another" commands of the New Testament. Though they work for every relationship, they are especially essential for marriage. I have highlighted a few that most couples will find are effective "tank fillers."

1. *Encourage and build up your mate.*

> *Therefore encourage one another and*
> *build each other up, just as you are doing.*
> 1 THESSALONIANS 5:11 ESV

As a pastoral counselor, I have met with many couples whose love tanks were so dry that they seemed incapable of speaking anything positive about each other. On more than one occasion, I've separated couples into two rooms and had each create a list of positive things they could say to the other. I have given them homework assignments: *tell your mate five positive things a day for the next week until our next session.* I have had them sit face-to-face, hold hands, and take turns affirming one another.

Some couples need a lot of prompting, so I'll have them list five to ten reasons why they were first attracted to each other and thought they would be good marriage partners. Then I'll have them list five to ten positive things they have heard someone else say about their mate, and then five to ten other positive things they could sincerely say about their mate.

Almost without exception, there will be tears and hugs before this exercise is done. It is amazing to think how many otherwise pretty good marriages are crumbling simply from one or both spouses neglecting to frequently, verbally, and positively encourage the other.

Sincere, positive, and encouraging comments will add to your mate's love tank. Negative, insincere, or discouraging comments, or not saying anything at all, will draw down your mate's love tank.

Let me strongly encourage you to make a list of your mate's positive qualities, things you especially appreciate. (This will improve your attitude toward your mate.) Next, be certain to mention a few of them to your mate each day as naturally as possible without acting as if you are doing an assignment or reading from a list. This affirmation and encouragement will definitely help your mate's attitude toward you.

2. *Honor your mate.*

> *Love one another with brotherly affection.*
> *Outdo one another in showing honor.*
> ROMANS 12:10 ESV

Honoring your mate is a matter of showing respect, admiration, deference, esteem, reverence, consideration, recognition, and appreciation. Honoring your mate is a matter of making him or her feel important.

It has been noted that "the deepest urge in human nature is the desire to feel important." Our spouses should come away from our interactions with them feeling valued instead of *de*valued. They should be very confident that they, and their opinions, matter deeply to us. They should always feel built up instead of torn down.

We must realize that the person who makes our mate feel most important will ultimately steal his or her heart. I want to be the man in my wife's life who makes her feel most appreciated, valued, and loved.

If you want to honor your spouse, practice walking into the room and saying, "There you are!" instead of, "Here I am." Learn to turn the spotlight on your spouse instead of on yourself. Honor your mate by focusing your attention and lifting him or her up with your words, attitudes, and actions.

Let me strongly encourage you this week to intentionally focus the majority of your conversations with your spouse on how he or she is feeling and what he or she is thinking or doing. This will definitely show your mate the honor he or she needs from you.

3. *Carry your mate's burdens.*

Carry each other's burdens, and in this way you will fulfill the law of Christ.
GALATIANS 6:2 NIV

All of us have difficult burdens to carry from time to time. The only thing more difficult than carrying a burden is trying to carry it alone. One of the reasons God gave us the gift of marriage was so we would not have to be alone or go through hardship alone.

In the phrase, "Carry each other's burdens," the word for "burden" speaks of "a load too big for one person to carry alone." The word used here for "carry" describes jointly putting your shoulder under someone else's heavy load. That is what you must be careful to do for your mate. By helping each other through tough times, the difficulties will draw you closer together instead of driving you further apart.

How can you help to carry your mate's burdens? Let me give you five suggestions:

1. Listen to him or her.
2. Pray *for* him or her.
3. Pray *with* him or her.
4. Give him or her a break for a time.
5. Help with a mundane task.

4. *Serve your mate.*

> *Do not use your freedom to indulge the flesh;*
> *rather, serve one another humbly in love.*
> GALATIANS 5:13 NIV

Serving is *doing what is needed when it is needed*. Serving one another is doing those little things that make the other person's life easier.

Cathy is great at serving me. She selflessly does the laundry, buys the groceries, fixes the meals, and cleans up afterward. She cleans the house, pays the bills, and manages everyone's doctor's appointments. Often she senses when I am especially busy or stressed at work, and she will go the extra mile to mow the grass or help me with a typing project. She always edits and proofreads the books I write. She constantly contributes to our relational love tank through her selfless service.

Several years ago I realized I was rather negligent at serving her in return. So I have been trying to do a better job of helping with the dishes or running the washing machine or picking something up at the store.

When the other person feels served, it adds to the love tank. When you only serve yourself, the love tank is depleted.

5. *Be sensitive to your mate.*

> *Get rid of all bitterness, rage and anger, brawling and slander, along with every form of malice. Be kind and compassionate to one another, forgiving each other, just as in Christ God forgave you.*
>
> EPHESIANS 4:31–32 NIV

In every relationship, including your marriage, you will get hurt. In a marriage, those hurts can be more frequent and more common, especially in the early years. This is because expectations are higher and we are around our mates more than anyone else, and in less guarded moments than on the job or at church. Often they say or do things that hurt us.

At that point we have a choice—and it is a *choice*, and not an automatic response. We can choose to become bitter and angry and deplete our relational tanks, or we can choose to be humble, sensitive, kindhearted, and compassionate, and thereby add to our love tanks.

The apostle Paul says, "Be kind and compassionate to one another." The problem occurs when we are sensitive to our *own* hurts and not to our mate's. Remember, it is usually hurt people who hurt people. If your spouse reflects some anger that he or she feels toward someone else by being irritable with you, don't take it personally and become embittered. Be sensitive to *why* he or she is hurting.

One Final Truth about Tank-Filling: I Cannot Fill My Spouse's Tank When Mine Is Empty

My neighbor Tony could not help me fill my lawn mower's gas tank because his gas can was empty. Likewise, I cannot fill Cathy's love tank if mine is empty. Even then, I can go to God to get my tank filled. My daily time with God allows Him to fill my tank, which enables me to fill the tanks of the people I love.

A Word of Caution

If, as you've read this chapter, you've been gathering ammunition to use against your spouse, then you've completely missed the point. Instead of thinking, *My spouse is supposed to fill my tank, and he or she is not doing a very good job*, ask yourself, "What am *I* doing to fill my spouse's love tank?"

Chapter 10

Connect with Your Mate's Heart

He gets me," she said with a warm smile. "I never felt as if my family understood me, but my husband understands me. And if there are times when he doesn't, he makes the effort to listen to me until he does."

These were the words of a very happy young wife explaining why she was so deeply in love with her husband. He obviously had learned how to unlock her heart.

"Even though he is ahead of me in some areas," she continued, "he never looks down on me. He lets me know that he recognizes and values what I bring to our marriage. Beyond that, whenever we struggle, he leads us back to God in prayer to get it worked out."

This wise husband was not using some new pop psychology technique. In fact, the advice he followed was nearly two thousand years old. It was written by the apostle Peter and is recorded in the Bible:

> *Husbands, likewise, dwell with them with understanding, giving honor to the wife, as to the weaker vessel, and as being heirs together of the grace of life, that your prayers may not be hindered.*
>
> 1 PETER 3:7 NKJV

In this powerful word of wisdom, Peter gives husbands the keys to deep connection with their wives. But these principles can work both ways, as well. Instead of focusing on whether you feel understood, work on understanding your spouse. Understand your spouse's weaknesses, respect your differences, and give him or her true honor.

Prayerfully recognize your linked spiritual heritage, equality, and mutual dependence on God's grace.

Secret #10
Connect with your spouse's heart.

Connect by Understanding

Peter advises husbands to connect with their wives by "dwelling with them with understanding." The key to unlocking your mate's heart is learning to listen so that he or she feels fully understood. Wise spouses push beyond mere communication to full *connection*. Let me suggest four aids in gaining deeper understanding of your mate.

1. *Talk less; listen more.*
Too often we think communication means *we're* talking. But in order to communicate effectively we must both talk *and* listen. If you don't listen, I can guarantee your spouse will feel misunderstood.

My dear brothers and sisters, take note of this: Everyone should be quick to listen, slow to speak and slow to become angry, because human anger does not produce the righteousness that God desires.
JAMES 1:19–20 NIV

Post this at all the intersections, dear friends: Lead with your ears, follow up with your tongue, and let anger straggle along in the rear.
JAMES 1:19–20 MSG

You may not always agree with everything your mate says, or understand what he or she feels. But that is not as important as making your spouse feel that you at least listened to what was communicated.

2. *Give your mate your full attention.*

It's very hard to be a good listener if you're not fully attending to what your mate is saying and feeling. Much of the time when people are speaking to us, our heads become filled with our own personal thoughts and agendas. We're so busy thinking of our response that we don't really hear what was said or take note of nonverbal cues.

To listen well, you must "be with" your mate. You must make eye contact while he or she is speaking. Try to engage with the words and the emotions being expressed. *Listen without thinking about how you're going to respond.*

Good listening cannot be accomplished when you're attending to your own inner thoughts instead of fully focusing on your mate. You may not always be able to stop such thoughts from occurring, but you can learn to put them aside for the moment and focus your attention on what is being said.

3. *Rewire yourself to learn.*

In counseling married couples, one theme I have seen repeatedly is that too many husbands and wives really don't know each other. Oh, they may know little habits and sayings, but they don't know their spouse's deep dreams or fears.

We need to become students of our mates. Get rid of the notion that you already know everything you need to know. Otherwise you won't discover what you've missed. You probably know a lot less about your mate than you think you do. If you will open your mind and look for the reasons behind your spouse's behavior, you'll take a big step toward connecting with his or her heart.

4. *Look for unspoken fears, concerns, moods, and aspirations.*

When people speak, they always reveal their deepest thoughts, ambitions, and concerns. Most of the time, however, neither the speaker nor the listener is aware of these subtle, underlying issues—but they are always there. Good listeners attend to unspoken emotions and concerns. By "reading between the lines," noticing subtle clues and empathizing with your mate's emotional foundation (either verbally or nonverbally), you can help him or her feel heard.

Connect by Honoring

Peter advises husbands to connect with their wives by "giving honor to [her], as to the weaker vessel." In other words, husbands, we are to esteem our wives very highly and treat them as we would a precious, priceless, fragile vase. When I tell men to treat their wives like a valuable vase, they tend to blink at me blankly, so allow me to give you several practical suggestions for connecting by honoring.

1. *See it from your mate's side.*

The notion of striving to see situations from the other person's side has been an immense help in every relationship I have, especially my marriage. Often the solution to disagreements comes when I try to understand the other side's perspective.

Spouses "feel felt" when we put ourselves in their shoes, look at the situation through their eyes, and try to feel the situation as they are feeling it.

2. *Show genuine interest.*

When possible, try to make your mate—including his or her feelings and interests—the center of your conversation. Look. Notice. Ask.

Your goal is to learn as much about your spouse as you can. Go into conversations realizing that there is something fascinating about your mate and try to discover it. Ask questions that demonstrate you want to know more. Ask questions that will cause your mate to talk about what he or she feels, thinks, or enjoys. Ask follow-up questions that show you heard and cared about what was said.

Here are a few questions that can lead to interesting and insightful conversations:

- "If you could change one thing about the direction of our marriage, what would it be?"
- "If there were one thing I could do to help you move more quickly toward your goals, what would it be?"
- "What's the one thing you're proudest of accomplishing?"
- "At this moment in your life (or in our marriage), what is your biggest fear?"

3. *Make your mate feel important.*

Mary Kay Ash began a successful corporation designed to allow women to advance by helping others succeed. She attributed much of her success to the idea that "everyone has an invisible sign hanging from their neck saying, 'Make me feel important.' "

Most of us don't feel very important or special. We're starving for attention. Your mate needs to matter to you. Satisfy that need.

4. *Express gratitude.*

Expressing gratitude is more than simply saying "thank you," although that is a big part of it. Gratitude deepens our relational connections when we thank others for something specific they did, acknowledge the effort they invested, and tell them the difference their actions made to us personally.

5. *Connect by Building Togetherness.*

Relationships are like diamonds. They have many facets. Often we get stuck focusing on only one side of connectedness, to the exclusion of the others. Wise couples build connections on as many sides and on as many levels as possible. These include the following:

- Sexual intimacy through physical affection
- Intellectual connectedness through sharing the world of ideas
- Creative unity built through sharing in creative acts
- Relational togetherness developed through shared experiences of fun and play
- Working connectedness by participating in tasks together
- Crisis intimacy that comes by going through hard issues, real problems, and pain together
- Conflict unity gained by facing and struggling through differences effectively together
- Spiritual intimacy gained by growing closer to god in an ongoing partnership

The eighth facet of connectedness—spiritual intimacy—is extremely important. Peter focuses on this when he encourages husbands to build connectedness by focusing on "being heirs together of the grace of life, that your prayers may not be hindered."

As we talked about in chapter 3, couples who pray together tend to stay together. Deep spiritual unity is developed between a husband and wife as they prayerfully recognize their linked spiritual heritage, their true spiritual equality, and their mutual dependence on God's grace.

Connect by Continuing to Date

Often love is spelled t-i-m-e. It is hard to feel close to your mate if you don't do things together. Good advice for any couple is to go on a date once a week. As Cathy and I were building a church and raising our children, we always knew that in our weekly date we would get at least one time a week to fully be together, catch up, and just talk. The more dates you have a week, the better it gets.

A good date does not have to be expensive. Over the years, we gathered ideas from friends and have enjoyed many cheap dates. Need some ideas? Here are several:

- Go on a walk in a park and eat fast food together on the way home.
- Browse in a bookstore—half the time together and the other half apart.
- Go to a play or a musical at a local community theater, high school, or college.

- Eat a simple, healthy dinner at home, and then go out for ice cream.
- Make a date to watch the sunset together from the back porch.
- Stay home and watch a movie snuggled up together on the couch.
- Play a board game together.
- Go to an old cemetery and search for the oldest and most interesting headstones.
- Attend a minor league baseball game.
- Double date with some good friends.
- Find a good, cheap restaurant you both like and be sure to eat there together once a month.
- Read the Sunday comics out loud to each other.
- Have a weekly date to watch the same TV show together.
- Go window shopping for something you can't afford now but hope to be able to buy in the future.
- Go to an interesting part of town, or a small town nearby, and bike or walk the streets together. Finish with dessert at a local shop.

Connect by Staying Loyal through a Tough Season

Strong marriages are the result of solid friendships. Such friendships are forged, and deep connections are developed, by remaining loyal in the face of great adversity.

A friend loves at all times, and is born, as is a brother, for adversity.
PROVERBS 17:17 AMP

Friends love through all kinds of weather.
PROVERBS 17:17 MSG

A friend is always a friend, and relatives are born to share our troubles.
PROVERBS 17:17 CEV

Note the phrase "at all times." A deep connection is developed through our commitment to love our mates at *all* times, including the tough times, the dull times, and the confusing times. Also note the word *adversity*. Real friends care about each other just as much during seasons of adversity as they do during seasons of prosperity. Note the phrase "is always a friend." That is what distinguishes a friend from an acquaintance. A friend runs to you when everyone else runs away. Friends are there "to share your troubles."

"Give Me a Gun"

After ten years of marriage, I was ill. . .very ill. I lost eighteen pounds in three weeks, which was a significant percentage of my body weight. I began to feel a terrible, steady pain in my joints and muscles. The slightest bit of cold air made it worse. I carried around a giant headache that would not go away.

My immune system went crazy and suddenly I was allergic to all sorts of things. My cognitive capacities sometimes short-circuited; I could see words in my head but had great difficulty getting them to come out of my mouth. (This is not a good thing if you're a pastor.) I could not sleep for more than a few hours at a time. Strangely, about five o'clock every evening, I would get a terrible sore throat.

None of that, however, could compare with the crushing fatigue I experienced. It felt like I was wearing concrete shoes and trying to run underwater. I woke up exhausted and stayed exhausted all day long. I would lie in bed and concentrate on mustering all of my strength just so I could turn over by myself. I had been a varsity athlete in college, and yet at one point I was so weak that the highlight of my day was crawling down the hall to the bathroom all by myself.

On top of that, my three boys were all under the age of five, and they could not understand why Dad couldn't play with them like he used to, or why he couldn't go out and make a snowman.

The severe pain and exhaustion went on week after week, month after month, year after year.

Eventually, I was diagnosed with chronic fatigue immune deficiency syndrome—CFIDS for short—among other things. (My male ego was hurt when I found out that CFIDS is most frequently contracted by women.) CFIDS at that time was an illness few people understood.

I was frustrated to be the slave of pain and fatigue. I was aggravated because I was a goal-oriented person who was now unable to pursue any goal other than survival. I was irritated because I did not have the strength to get off the couch to play with my boys. I was discouraged because my fatigue was wearing out my wife.

I couldn't see how I could go on like this. I felt as if everyone would be much better off without me, and I would be in heaven and out of pain.

Every night about nine o'clock, depression would fall on me like a ton of bricks. Cathy would ask, "Is there anything I can get you?" I found myself saying, "Yes, bring me a gun. I want to put every-one out of their misery." This morbid scene played itself out night after night.

Yet, through it all, Cathy never got mad at me. She maintained a positive attitude. She did not complain about all the extra work my illness caused her.

It took me nearly eight years to see CFIDS defeated in my life. Physically, I had to totally and radically reorient my life around a very strict diet, ardent daily exercise, getting enough rest, managing stress, and regular detoxification. Spiritually, I learned to live a life of deeper gratitude and faith. Emotionally, I rediscovered my identity in Christ and used journaling to manage my emotions.

Through it all, Cathy loved me loyally. She loved me through the bad times. She was a friend through the adversity. As a result, a connection was created and a bond was forged that is unbreakable to this day. After all we've been through together, it's no surprise she's my best friend.

Chapter 11

Resolve Conflict

have seen the scene reenacted dozens of times. A married couple calls for a counseling appointment. Before they come in, I move the two chairs in front of my desk right next to each other.

A few minutes later, the secretary lets the couple into my office. The tension is already thick between them. The first thing they do is move the chairs farther apart.

After the preliminaries, they tell me why they are unhappy with each other. When I have filled a sheet of legal paper with the issues of conflict and have highlighted what appear to be the major issues, I encourage them that their marriage is not hopeless. Then I explain two fundamental concepts: the Wall of Resentment and the Garden of Marital Love.

The Wall of Resentment

In any relationship between two imperfect people who are of different genders, come from different backgrounds and families, with distinct personalities, living in a fallen world, conflict and pain are inevitable. Whether the hurts are caused intentionally or inadvertently, they still hurt. If these conflicts go unresolved, they harden into "bricks" that form an invisible "wall of resentment" between a husband and wife. Every incident of unresolved resentment becomes a separate brick. After years of unresolved conflict, the bricks form a thick wall.

I often tell couples that, even though I cannot literally see the wall of resentment between them, I can feel it from the moment they walk into my office. I see it as they pull their chairs apart and hear it in their litany of complaints. It obviously keeps them from seeing each other's needs and hearing each other's heart. This barrier of bitterness clearly hinders the good they do for each other and the love they have for each other. If such a wall is allowed to stand, it will eventually chill the love out of the relationship.

The Garden of Love

After explaining the Wall of Resentment, I often discuss the Garden of Marital Love. Every marriage begins as a new garden, with tender plants of love, trust, and hope. But every time conflict comes, or a relationship sin such as neglect, insensitivity, or harshness occurs, it's as if weeds are being sown in the garden. If the weeds are allowed to remain, they will grow fast and strong. If love, trust, and hope are not carefully nurtured, the weeds will soon overtake them. The garden that began with so much promise becomes an ugly mess.

Secret #11
Remove resentments and resolve conflicts.

Essentials for Pulling Down Walls and Pulling Out Weeds

King David had a covenant relationship with God. He broke the covenant through sin. His sin created a separating wall between him and God (Isaiah 59:1–2). In Psalm 51, David does his part to tear down the wall by confessing his sin. In this psalm of repentance, we find four steps for pulling down relational barriers: humility, sensitivity, reconciliation, and restoration. Each step can be captured in a three-word statement that expresses an essential attitude for resolving conflict and removing relational roadblocks.

1. *Humility: "I was wrong."*

> *For I know my transgressions and my sin is ever before me. Against You, You only, **I have sinned** and done what is evil in Your sight, so that You are justified when You speak and blameless when You judge.*
>
> PSALM 51:3–4 NASB (EMPHASIS ADDED)

"I have sinned." David removed the relational roadblock between himself and God because he did not make excuses. He did not rationalize. He honestly admitted his responsibility. He confessed his sin.

Pride is probably the biggest barrier to making relationships right. When no one will admit to being wrong, invisible walls are constructed. For example, a story is told of an elderly couple who had such a bitter disagreement that they stopped talking to each other, even though they continued to use the same rooms and sleep in the same bed. A chalk line divided their living space into two halves, separating doorway and fireplace, so that each could come and go and get their own meals without trespassing on the other's domain. In the black of night, each could hear the other breathing. For years, they coexisted in grinding silence. Neither was willing to take the first step of reconciliation.

That may seem like a funny picture, but I've encountered several marriages that essentially operate the same way—two people living together behind invisible barriers. Their pride maintains the wall.

Hosts of family problems. . .could be improved by the use of four simple words: "You may be right. . ." People who apologize are not vacillating. You must have a certain moral certitude to admit you are wrong. Because relationships are the most difficult things we attempt in this life, of *course* we will make mistakes in them. And when we do, we can save ourselves considerable misery by apologizing.[1]

So often, when there are relationship conflicts, we want to defend ourselves. Think about that: *defend ourselves*. The very words conjure images of walls and weapons. The bigger the attack, the more defensive we get. Humility has a wonderful way of disarming potential problems.

I ask husbands and wives to own their part of the wall. I usually start with the easiest brick. Maybe his part was being insensitive and her part was getting over-the-top angry about it. I ask the husband to hold his wife's hands, look her in the eye, and say, "When I did such and such, *I was wrong*."

When he is sincere, her defenses begin to come down. The ice begins to melt. The brick is loosened. The weed has been identified. We're making progress, but we're not done yet.

2. Sensitivity: "I am sorry."

Against You, You only, I have sinned and done what is evil in Your sight, so that You are justified when You speak and blameless when You judge.

PSALM 51:4 NASB

Reread the verse above. Note how many times David uses the word *you*.

He was able to reconcile his relationship with God because he started with humility and proceeded with sensitivity. He did not rationalize his behavior from his own perspective. He identified how his actions had affected God—*You, You, Your, You, You*. In essence he says, "I realize that my sin has hurt *you* and *I am sorry*."

Our mates not only *want* us to humbly own our part of the conflict, they *need* us to be sensitive to their needs and hurts. They need us to give them sympathy. They have a legitimate need to be understood and recognized.

Conflicts tend to intensify if we feel as if the other person is making no effort to understand us. If you misspeak or accidently hurt your spouse, it can easily become the seed of an ugly weed *if* he or she feels as if you don't care. A true apology is more than just acknowledgment of a mistake. It is recognition that something you have said or done has damaged your relationship—and that you *care* enough about the relationship to want it repaired and restored.

I must admit that during the first few years of my marriage, I would hurt Cathy and not even realize it. I was too selfish and insensitive. I've had to work hard to become sensitive to the effect that my tone, my words, my humor, my teasing, and my decisions may have on Cathy's feelings.

It's amazing how the attitude we project to others is often the attitude we receive in return. If we bring sincere humility and sensitivity, they usually respond with openness, humility, and sensitivity. If we come with arrogant pride and anger, we usually get pride and defensive anger in return. As I ask married couples to own their parts of the wall, I press them to not only admit their wrongs but also to express sensitivity. I prompt them to say, "I am sorry." So many times I've seen the other spouse (usually the wife) begin to melt and tear up when one spouse humbly and sensitively says, "I now realize how my actions must have hurt you. I am so sorry." At this point, the icy wall between the two melts noticeably.

3. Reconciliation: "Please forgive me."

Be gracious to me, O God, according to Your lovingkindness; according to the greatness of Your compassion blot out my transgressions. Wash me thoroughly from my iniquity and cleanse me from my sin.

PSALM 51:1–2 NASB

"Blot out my transgressions," "wash me," "cleanse me from my sin." Sincere humility and expressed sensitivity go a long way toward removing relational barriers, but when the resentments are caused by sin, nothing less than asking for forgiveness will lead to reconciliation.

The word *forgive* means "to pardon; to cancel a debt; to blot out an offense." David openly asks for God's forgiveness: "Have mercy on me," "blot out my transgressions," "wash me," "cleanse me."

I find that it's usually not enough to simply admit our sin (humility) and acknowledge the hurt it has caused others (sensitivity). We also need to ask for forgiveness (reconciliation).

Have you ever had dandelions in your yard? Failing to ask for forgiveness is like seeing a dandelion in the center of your lawn and simply walking away. Later you wonder why your entire yard is filled with dandelions. It's because you left the weed and it has spread. Pulling the head off a dandelion won't stop it. You must pull the weed out at the roots. The way to pull out relational dandelions is by asking for forgiveness. Merely saying "I apologize" is usually insufficient. It breaks the weed off but doesn't get to the root. Resentments that are glossed over will likely grow back.

As I ask married couples to own their parts of the resentment wall, I press them to not only admit their wrongs and express sensitivity but also to say, "Please forgive me." Those three words acknowledge the seriousness of the offense and seek resolution. When forgiveness is sincerely asked for and given, you can feel the wall shake as a foundational brick is removed.

As relational bricks are progressively addressed and removed, it's amazing to see the couple start to lean closer to each other. They take each other's hands as I continue to talk. They may even hug and kiss at this point.

But they aren't done yet.

4. Restoration: "I forgive you" and "I love you."

Let me hear joy and gladness; let the bones you have crushed rejoice. Hide your face from my sins and blot out all my iniquity. . . . Do not cast me from your presence or take your Holy Spirit from me. Restore to me the joy of your salvation and grant me a willing spirit, to sustain me.

PSALM 51:8–12 NIV

After David had confessed his sin and asked for forgiveness, he wanted more than a legal pardon. He wanted a restored and reconciled relationship. He needed God to forgive him and reaffirm His love for him.

If we go back to our example of the dandelions, giving forgiveness and confirming love is like spraying the yard with weed killer, and then, after they all die, covering the area with fertilizer, which nourishes and strengthens the lawn to keep the weeds from returning. We need forgiveness to kill the weeds and love to fertilize the lawn.

When someone sincerely asks for forgiveness, only three words will suffice in response: "I forgive you." If our mates have sincerely humbled themselves, expressed sensitivity, and asked for forgiveness, the least we can do is give it. Forgiveness should be given as quickly and completely as possible. For small offenses, it can be granted very quickly. Larger, deeper hurts will obviously take more time.

People who refuse to forgive don't see themselves realistically. Though hanging onto a grudge may give us a feeling of satisfaction, we ultimately hurt ourselves more than we hurt others. Refusing to forgive cancels the mercy and grace in own lives.

I often hear people talk about their inability to fully forgive. They say, "I'll forgive, but I'll never forget." Of course it is difficult to wipe away a crushing pain. Yet that must be our desire. We must remember that forgiving and forgetting are not *feelings*—they're choices we must make. We can choose to extend forgiveness even before we feel like it. And we can choose not to dwell on past offenses.

Often one spouse or the other will genuinely struggle to forgive. Yet while I can understand their dilemma, it does not excuse their holding onto bitterness. When we do not have it within ourselves to forgive, we must turn to God and rely on His grace to give us the ability to forgive. Notice Paul's words to the Ephesian church:

*Let all bitterness, wrath, anger, clamor, and evil speaking be put away from you, with all malice. And be kind to one another, tenderhearted, forgiving one another, **even as God in Christ forgave you**.*

EPHESIANS 4:31–32 NKJV (EMPHASIS ADDED)

A Confession

A few years ago, Cathy and I encountered a large wall of resentment between us. She was cool and distant, and it bugged me. At first, I wanted to put the blame on her; but God reminded me that solutions start when we acknowledge our own part. So I asked Him to show me my part of the problem.

As I read the Bible—I happened to be reading in Psalms—I realized that Cathy was resentful because I had hurt her. Several little things had taken root like weeds and were beginning to choke the love out of our marriage.

I bought her a nice card and wrote a note inside. The note had five paragraphs. In the first paragraph, I told her I loved her and was committed to her and our marriage. The second section began with the words, "I was wrong," and I named every possible thing I could think of that might have hurt her. In the third paragraph, I wrote, "I am sorry," and I told her that I was sorry for the ways my actions and words had hurt her. The fourth paragraph began, "Please forgive me." The last paragraph simply reaffirmed how much I loved her.

Writing that note was a hard thing to do. I could have been puffy and proud—and I'd be a very lonely guy. Instead, I acknowledged the problem. I admitted to everything I could. I asked for forgiveness and expressed my love.

Did it work?

Yes, in several ways, both direct and indirect.

First, it set me free from resentment and guilt.

Second, it elicited a response from Cathy. She took responsibility for some weeds she had allowed to take root in the garden of our marriage in response to the pain I had caused her.

Third, it opened a hole in the wall of resentment and allowed us to be reconciled and restored. Then we made up. (By the way, making up was a great deal of fun.)

An Observation

God says that no matter who causes a problem in a relationship, both parties are to take steps to resolve it (Matthew 5:23–25). Fairness and fault are not the issue. What's important is taking the initiative to be reconciled (Matthew 18:15).

A Suggestion

If you and your spouse have an area of conflict that you just can't resolve, consider enlisting a third party to help you.

Look in the Mirror

Ask yourself these questions:

- Is there distance in your relationship with your mate?
- Without accusing your mate, what problem can *you* own and admit?

- Where have *you* been insensitive to your mate's feelings?
- What do *you* need to ask forgiveness for?
- What do you need to forgive?
- Will you reaffirm your love?
- Will you do your part to tear down any and all relational walls and pull out every relational weed?

Notes
1. Alan Loy McGinnis, *The Friendship Factor: How to Get Closer to the People You Care For*, twenty-fifth anniversary revised and expanded edition (Minneapolis: Augsburg, 2004), 158–159.

Chapter 12

Fight Fair

Two men were talking at work. One said, "I had a fight with my wife last night."

"Really," the other replied. "How'd it end up?"

The first man smiled. "It ended up with her crawling to me on her hands and knees."

"Really?" the other man exclaimed. "What did she say?"

The first man looked a little sheepish and said, "Well, she said, 'Come out from under the bed and fight like a man.' "

I hope your marital conflicts don't end the same way!

Conflict within marriage is inevitable. If a couple doesn't learn how to fight or disagree successfully, their marriage will inevitably suffer.

Though conflict is inevitable, it does not have to be devastating. Successful conflict resolution has certain rules that make it *instructive* and *constructive* rather than *destructive*. If you learn to "fight fair," conflict will actually strengthen your relationship.

Secret #12
Learn to fight fair.

In his letter to the Ephesians, the apostle Paul gives insights that will help us make conflict resolution a positive experience.

Therefore each of you must put off falsehood and speak truthfully to your neighbor, for we are all members of one body. "In your anger do not sin": Do not let the sun go down while you are still angry, and do not give the devil a foothold. Anyone who has been stealing must steal no longer, but must work, doing something useful with their own hands, that they may have something to share with those in need. Do not let any unwholesome talk come out of your mouths, but only what is helpful for building others up according to their needs, that it may benefit those who listen. And do not grieve the Holy Spirit of God, with whom you were sealed for the day of redemption. Get rid of all bitterness, rage and anger, brawling and slander, along with every form of malice. Be kind and compassionate to one another, forgiving each other, just as in Christ God forgave you.

EPHESIANS 4:25–32 NIV

In these verses, we can see that unfair fighting results in sin, giving the devil a foothold and grieving the Holy Spirit, as well as bitterness, rage, anger, brawling, slander, and malice. All of which will ruin a marriage. In order to avoid these ugly outcomes, we must apply the rules of fighting fair.

How to Fight Fair

1. *Be honest.*

Therefore, putting away lying, "Let each one of you speak truth with his neighbor," for we are members of one another.

EPHESIANS 4:25 NKJV

Intimacy is determined by honesty. The first aspect of fighting fair is being honest. Marital honesty involves two sides of the same coin.

First, *stop lying*. When conflict is evident, mates can lie to each other in several ways. They may lie by avoidance. When she asks what is wrong, he sighs and lies, "Oh, nothing." Or she may lie by deflection. When he asks her, "What's wrong?" she lies and replies, "I'm just tired."

These little lies result from a desire to avoid conflict. The reason we avoid conflict is because we believe it tears down a relationship and causes divorce. Yet, in reality, one of the prime predictors of divorce is the habitual *avoidance* of conflict.[1]

Too many marriages become like the cartoon in which a couple explains to the marriage counselor, "We never talk anymore. We figured out that's when we do all our fighting."

In the beginning, most couples avoid conflict because they're in love and they believe that agreeing is part of "staying in love." They're afraid that if they disagree—or fight—they'll ruin their marriage. They believe that, if they are truly "in love," they'll agree about most things, especially the important things. Later, they avoid conflict because when they try to resolve issues, it is handled poorly and the fights become destructive and painful. So they end up trying to avoid conflict at all costs. But conflict avoidance—and the lying that inevitably goes with it—is actually an impediment to a strong marriage.

Second, *speak the truth*. Wise couples learn to be honest with each other. They refrain from exaggerating, fabricating, or glossing over significant details in their lives. They are also appropriately honest about their feelings. Failure to be honest is destructive to any relationship.

In a counseling course I took, the professor told of a man who was severely depressed and went to see a Christian counselor. He had been through shock therapy, group therapy, psychoanalysis, and had even been institutionalized for a short time. Finally, he got honest. The truth was that he had never wanted to marry his wife. He had done so only to please his mother. He had kept this lie inside for twenty-two years.

The counselor helped him face the issue and appropriately tell his wife, who of course had already sensed as much. Because they believed in marriage as a covenant with God, they went to God and the Word in order to better fulfill their responsibilities to one another. Within a surprisingly short amount of time, they were feeling and behaving like newlyweds.

In another case, something was eating at the wife. Inside, she was very upset with her husband, and it went on for months. Finally, they went to see a counselor together.

Once they were seated, she angrily blurted out, "I am sure my husband is cheating on me. He has not been bringing home his overtime pay, and I want to know who he's spending it on."

The husband smiled shyly and reached into his coat pocket. He opened his wallet and inside was all the money. "It's all here, dear," he said. "I've been saving it to buy you something special for our twenty-fifth anniversary."

2. Stay Controlled.

> "In your anger do not sin": Do not let the sun go down while you are still angry, and do not give the devil a foothold.
>
> EPHESIANS 4:26–27 NIV

Unresolved anger results in sin and gives the devil a foothold. From this place of operation in your marriage, resentments are created, relational weeds are sown, and marital walls are built.

Paul indicates that anger is inevitable. But he commands us to keep it from becoming *sinful.* The difference between sinful anger and righteous indignation is a matter of motive, amount, delivery, and outcome.

Paul's advice is to avoid sinful anger by resolving our disputes quickly. Sinful anger is typically expressed in one of two ways—clamming up or blowing up. *Clamming up*—or anger turned inward—depresses the person who is holding things in. Eventually, this inner anger explodes in ugly and exaggerated ways.

The more obvious expression of sinful anger is *blowing up.* Yelling and throwing things don't resolve the problem; they only add to the conflict and make it sinful and destructive.

Yet blowing up is not limited to loud yelling and throwing things. After studying marriages for twenty years, John Gottman found several predictors of divorce.[2] One involved beginning conversations with criticism, sarcasm, or harsh words. Another is what he calls "flooding," which involves dumping so much negativity into a discussion that you leave your mate shell-shocked and disengaged from the conversation—and ultimately from the relationship.

Gottman found that, during conflict discussions, the ratio of positive to negative interactions in relationships headed for divorce is 0.8:1. In stable and happy marriages, the ratio of positive to negative is 5:1.

When dealing with conflict, the tone we use is important. Our tone creates the atmosphere that either escalates or eases the problem.

A soft answer turns away wrath,
but a harsh word stirs up anger.

PROVERBS 15:1 NKJV

Sometimes, in our anger, we use words that by their very nature ignite the level of tension in the conflict. Fair fighting requires both parties to diligently avoid using words that pour fuel on the fire.

Avoid Gunpowder Words

Exaggerations and absolutes: *most, least, worst, biggest,* "you *always,*" "you *never*"

Derogatory or sarcastic labels or names: *spoiled brat, nut, wimp, jerk, creep, prom queen, diva, big hero*

Comparisons: "Sarah's husband always. . ." "Josh's wife would never. . ."

Sideswipe words or indirect attacks: "Most husbands take out the trash. . . ." "Seventy-five percent of the wives in America would agree with me. . . ."

Defensive attacking responses: "What about *you*?" "The only reason I ever do that is because you. . ."

Manipulative threats: "If you do that again, I'm leaving. . ." "If that's the way you want it, I'll never _____ again."

3. *Seek resolution.*

Do not let the sun go down while you are still
angry, and do not give the devil a foothold.

EPHESIANS 4:26–27 NIV

The idea of not allowing the sun to go down on your anger is all about seeking resolution. In concert with what we discussed in chapter 11, let me suggest several steps that greatly aid in conflict resolution and relational reconciliation.

First, *acknowledge that a problem exists*. Too many couples go too long avoiding conflict. When this happens, a backlog of frustration develops that almost always leads to an ugly explosion. Therefore, when you start to become frustrated with your mate, or when you sense that he or she is becoming frustrated with you, say these simple words: "It seems we have a problem." Notice the word *we*. Saying to your mate "*You* have a problem" may feel like an attack or criticism.

Second, *be careful to attack the problem, not the person*. When conflict resolution attempts are unsuccessful, it is often because one person feels attacked. The key to resolving conflict is making your mate feel esteemed and valued.

For example, when conflict begins, one spouse should calmly say something like this: "I love you, I care about you, I'm committed to you, but this situation we're facing needs to be resolved. Let's put our heads together and see if we can come up with a good solution that works for both of us." In this way, instead of shooting each other across the table, the couple joins together and focuses their combined energies on solving the problem.

Third, *admit your share of the problem*. Jesus told us to be careful to take the beam out of our own eye before we complain about the speck in someone else's (Matthew 7:3–5). Try to see how your actions or words may have created or added to the conflict. Be the first to admit your share of the problem.

Fourth, as we discussed in the previous chapter, *ask for forgiveness.* Don't underestimate the power of saying, "I was wrong," "I am sorry," "Please forgive me," and "I love you."

Resolutions Commands to Remember

1. *Thou shalt learn to fight fair and resolve conflicts.* Successful couples know how to contain their disagreements and keep them from spilling over and contaminating the rest of their relationship.
2. *Thou shalt not attempt to solve a conflict at the wrong time.* It is usually ineffective to try to solve a serious conflict when you only have a couple of minutes or if you are out in public or when you are exhausted.
3. *Thou shalt not blame your emotions, attitudes, actions, words, or reactions on someone else.* Be responsible for your part of the conflict.
4. *Thou shalt not replay the same old arguments.* Persistent disagreements reveal that the real issue has not yet been resolved. If you're fighting over the same things time after time, seek some outside, objective help to resolve the conflict.
5. *Thou shalt deal with only one problem at a time.* Don't wait until you can't stand it anymore and then dump a dozen frustrations on your mate all at once. That's simply not fair.
6. *Thou shalt deal in the present, not the past.* Don't keep dredging up old wounds. I'm sure you've heard the story of the man who went to a psychologist and pleaded, "Doctor, you've got to help me!"

"What's wrong?" the doctor asked.

"It's my wife," the man said. "She's historical."

"You mean *hysterical*," the doctor replied.

"No," the man said, "I mean *historical*. She remembers every wrong thing I've ever done."

The reason this story has hung around for so many years is that it contains truth. Too often we waste energy fighting past battles instead of resolving present conflicts.

4. *Build bridges, not walls.*

> *Do not let any unwholesome talk come out of your mouths,*
> *but only what is helpful for building others up according to their needs,*
> *that it may benefit those who listen. And do not grieve the Holy Spirit*
> *of God, with whom you were sealed for the day of redemption.*
> EPHESIANS 4:29–30 NIV

Unproductive words grieve God's Holy Spirit. They cause Him to hurt for us and for the ones we hurt with our words. Unhelpful words will also pollute our marriages.

Remember, words are like toothpaste—once they've been squeezed out, they can't be put back. Therefore, we need to be careful to use our words to build bridges rather than walls with our mates.

There is never a good time for unproductive words. This is especially true when seeking to resolve conflict. We must eradicate all foul or polluting language, every evil or unwholesome word, and all worthless comments from our conversations. Our vocabulary must be scrubbed clean of every corrupt, rotten, worthless, unwholesome, destructive, cutting, critical, cruel, condemning, or sarcastic comment, because they only build walls of resentment.

But, you say, "How can I cut out the cutting remarks?"

Paul emphasizes that the key to putting off bad behavior is to practice good behavior—replace lying with honesty, stealing with hard work and generosity, and bitterness with love. Thus, the way to stop using unproductive words is to strive valiantly to use only productive, affirming, uplifting words.

In dealing with conflict, choose words that edify (build up) your mate and create avenues to his or her heart. Paul describes such words as helpful and necessary—which would include words of affirmation ("good job," "thank you"), acceptance ("no matter what," "I will always love you"), attention ("I noticed the extra effort you put into dinner," "I saw that you cleaned the garage"), and affection ("I love you").

When I was growing up, my father taught me a three-pronged test for selecting the right words for every situation: "Is it true? Is it kind? Is it necessary?" Of course, when he rebuked me for using unproductive words, I always replied, "But it's true." Then he would remind me that along with being true it also had to be kind and necessary.

5. *Cancel bitterness.*

Get rid of all bitterness, rage and anger, brawling and slander, along with every form of malice. Be kind and compassionate to one another, forgiving each other, just as in Christ God forgave you.
EPHESIANS 4:31–32 NIV

Unresolved bitterness never disappears on its own. Unchecked, it always grows and breeds ugly relationship killers such as indignation, resentment, quarreling, slander, abusive language, spite, ill will, and the desire to injure.

Beyond that, bitterness is entirely unproductive. It is like drinking poison and expecting the other person to die. It is like a cancer that eats you up on the inside, robbing you of joy and life. It also is a marriage killer.

Paul encourages us to forcibly banish bitterness from our hearts before it takes root and grows. He also gives us a recipe for success: "Be kind and compassionate to one another, forgiving each other, just as in Christ God forgave you."

Be kind: When we approach every conflict with kindness—in our words, attitudes, and actions—God has a wonderful way of eradicating bitterness from our hearts. It also helps keep the door open for resolution.

Be compassionate: This literally means be "loving hearted." It speaks of approaching conflict with an attitude that is tenderhearted, sensitive, merciful, and understanding. If we try to look at the conflict from our mates' perspective, and by being sensitive to their concerns, it aids in solving the conflict and reduces the chances of our becoming embittered.

Be forgiving of each other: It is helpful to recognize that forgiveness is an active choice that leads to a feeling, not a feeling that leads to a choice. When we're in the midst of a conflict, we don't feel like forgiving. God knows this and does not ask us to *feel* forgiveness; instead, He tells us to *choose* forgiveness. Choosing to forgive is choosing not to mention the offense to God, myself, or others again. It is choosing to treat the other person as if the offense had never occurred. This is not easy. So how do we do it?

Forgive just as in Christ God forgave you: Because of what Jesus did for us, God chose to unconditionally pardon us for countless offenses. He extended to us the undeserved, frequent, supernatural cancellation of the debt for our sins. Because He loves us, He has chosen to delete the records of all we have done to hurt Him.

Sometimes our mate hurts us so deeply that our human capacity for forgiveness is not sufficient. We just don't have it within ourselves to forgive. The only way we can forgive is by choosing to offer supernatural forgiveness; that is, taking the unconditional forgiveness that God has extended to us and choosing to extend it to the one who has wronged us.

When the wound is extremely large or deep, it will probably need to be completely opened in order for it to be healed. The process of choosing to forgive by appropriating God's supernatural forgiveness may come slowly. Be patient. It can and will occur.

A Final Thought

Use the inevitable conflicts of life to draw closer to your mate, not further apart. Make the effort to be honest about conflict and approach it with self-control. Work toward resolution and use conflict to build bridges, not walls. Replace bitterness with active love.

Notes

1. Diane Sollee, "The number one predictor of divorce. . ."
http://www.smartmarriages.com/divorcepredictor.html
2. John Gottman, "What is 'dysfunctional' when a relationship is ailing?"
http://www.gottmancouplesretreats.com/about/relationships-dysfunctional-divorce-predictors.aspx

Conclusion:

Suggestions for a More Effective Marriage

Congratulations!

You have reached the end of the book, but your journey to a better marriage doesn't end here. Let me remind you that information without application leads to self-delusion (see James 1:22–25). Your marriage will not improve just because you read the information in this book—or any other book, for that matter. Your marriage will only improve as you *apply* what you have learned.

Let me suggest that you look back through this book, noting the things you underlined. Prayerfully ask God to work these secrets into your life. Determine to put into practice what you have learned.

If you have not yet done so, reread the book with your mate or mate-to-be. Take it a chapter at a time, at most. Take turns reading aloud. Stop after each section and discuss what you think about it, how you feel about it, and how you can apply it.

If you have not yet done so, read and discuss this book as part of a small group.

Meet with a group of other couples or couples-to-be. Study one chapter a week for fourteen weeks. Discuss how you are striving to put these truths into practice.

What do you have to lose? Or, more important, what do you stand to gain?

Made in the USA
Columbia, SC
01 July 2018